I0167630

SABINE MACDONALD

THE WHISPERING BUTTERFLY

PLATYPUS
PUBLISHING

This book is dedicated
to all adventurers
in search for their treasure

Contents

Acknowledgments

Maya came alive because I dared to write her. But she stayed alive because of you.

Thank you to all my friends, colleagues, and family who walked with me through the highs and the lows, who held space for the chaos and the clarity, and who never stopped believing. But a special thank you goes to those of you who made my life uncomfortable, uneasy, and wildly challenging. Without you, I wouldn't have grown the way I did. Without you, Maya would have never seen the light of day. You were a gift. One I didn't ask for but, without knowing it at the time, deeply needed.

Writing this book was its own wild adventure. Some chapters were delightful. Others felt like open-heart surgery without anesthesia. Reliving some moments was brutal. Facing the fear of overwhelm (yet again) was a full experience in itself. I couldn't have done it without my book accountability partners: Emily Tell and Colby Balch. We kept each other motivated, inspired, and just sane enough to finish.

Once Maya's story was written, I handed her off, nervously, to a circle of brave souls who offered bold, honest feedback. Thank you to Jorge Theresin, Stephanie Shreve, Erika Rummel, Gustavo Bijl, Dorothy Bosse, Diane Wolf, Roland Schulze, Maureen McLean, Jack Tannerya, Patricia Garcia, Meryl Schroyen, and Eike Croucher. Because of you, this story became clearer, deeper, and stronger. Thanks to their early belief, Maya already has fans across Honduras, the U.S., Canada, the Netherlands, Germany, Spain, Belgium, and Australia. I'll admit, I was terrified to hear their verdict. Because I knew they'd be honest. And yet, their reflections moved me to tears. They gave me the courage to keep going. To bring Maya fully into the world. To offer this story in the hope that it might help someone else reclaim a joy they thought they'd lost.

Here are a few words from them that moved me deeply:

> *"I found myself in Maya's shoes so many times..."*
>
> *"I've been listening to my clients tell me that they don't know 'who they are anymore' and I kept thinking, they HAVE to read your book!"*
>
> *"There are many, many women (and probably men too) who will need to read this story, and give themselves permission to dream that a new way of showing up is possible for them."*
>
> *"I read it in one sitting. I did not move. It drew me in immediately and did not let me go. Maya's growth and empowerment was so complete it challenged my own thinking."*
>
> *"Your story is relatable and important!"*
>
> *"It makes change seem available to anyone."*
>
> *"It's so vivid and beautifully written, with one-liners so powerful."*
>
> *"I loved your book!"*
>
> *"Thank you so much for sharing."*

To my family: thank you.

Especially to my husband, Peter MacDonald, who gave me the freedom, space, and patience to write this book through quiet hours and chaotic days. Thank you for trusting that this mattered. I know it wasn't always easy. But if this book touches even one life, if just one person finds hope in these pages, it was worth every moment.

And now, a note to someone I rarely thank: *me*.

Thank you, self, for saying yes to this dream that lived in a dusty corner of your heart for over a decade. For showing up. For finishing. I'm proud of myself for finally checking off the box that said: "Write a book."

And last, but not least, thank you, dear reader.

You picked up this book. You turned the first page. You said yes to Maya. And maybe you said yes to yourself with all your heart. As you read, may you hear the whisper of your own transformation. And when the final page turns, may your wings feel ready, because butterflies don't go back into cocoons. They fly.

Enjoy the journey!

I

THE FALL

"You were born with wings.
Why prefer to crawl through life?"
Rumi

.

1

MISSION IMPOSSIBLE

Monday morning. 6:00 AM.

The alarm buzzed, a shrill sound that drilled into Maya's skull. It felt even more annoying than usual, as if the universe had cranked up the volume just to spite her. Her bed, on the other hand, had never been more comfortable, warm, and safe. An escape from reality. It seemed an impossible mission to get out of bed, especially on Mondays.

Five more minutes. She thought to herself and reached blindly for the snooze button, a well-practiced move, a ritual at this point. Five more minutes to pretend that Monday didn't exist. Five more minutes to delay stepping onto the battlefield of life.

Why was getting out of bed always so damn hard? Especially on Mondays? The world in bed was peaceful. No meetings. No emails. No boss breathing down her neck. Just warmth, silence, and the promise of peace. But just as she drifted back into the depths of her dreamworld, the alarm shrieked again, yanking her back into the cold clutches of reality.

Time to get up. Time to fight through another week. With a groan, Maya forced herself to move, her body feeling as if it had doubled in weight overnight. Every muscle protested as she swung her legs over the edge of the bed. The moment her foot touched the floor, the cold seeped through her skin, sending a shiver up her spine. Yawning, she ran a hand through her tangled hair, blinking at the mess that surrounded her. Dirty clothes were scattered across the floor, dishes were stacked precariously on the coffee table, wilting plants drooped in surrender, and a fine layer of dust coated the furniture. The apartment was a disaster zone. She had meant to clean up over the weekend, but instead, she had spent the entire time working to finalize and rehearse the presentation for the board meeting. The rest of her time, she sprawled on the couch, numbly scrolling through social media and flipping through TV channels without really watching.

She turned to the window, which was streaked with grime. Outside, heavy snowflakes drifted down from the sky.

Great. Just what I needed. Maya thought. Snow meant delays. Traffic jams. More stress. If she didn't hurry, she'd be late again. And today, of all days, she couldn't afford that.

One glance at her calendar made her stomach tighten. Back-to-back meetings. No breathing room. Not even enough time to sneak to the restroom between them. And the first one? A board meeting. While staring at her phone, she saw that her inbox already signaled 75 new incoming emails for today, and the internal company messaging tool still had 250 pending unread messages. 50 more than yesterday night. She completely lost control of what was happening to her.

Brilliant. Just the way to start a week.

But first things first. Maya shuffled into the kitchen, her limbs still half-asleep, her brain unwilling to engage until one crucial task was complete. Making coffee. The one thing standing between her and a complete breakdown. She prepared the machine, and the comforting gurgle of brewing coffee filled the silence. A rich, familiar aroma drifted through the air, curling around her like a warm embrace, promising functionality throughout the day.

While the machine continued running, she trudged into the bathroom and stepped under the shower, an icy jet of water blasted against her skin, making her gasp.

Jesus Christ! She fumbled with the knob, but the water barely warmed beyond lukewarm today.

Shivering, she rushed through the shower, barely rinsing the shampoo out of her hair before grabbing a towel and darting toward her closet. Now for the next daily struggle: choosing what to wear.

As the only woman in the boardroom, appearances mattered. She needed to look sharp. Professional. Unshakable. She held up a few options, frowning. Blue or green? Red or purple?

Why can't we all just wear uniforms? Life would be so much simpler.

Settling on a crisp white shirt, black trousers, and her favorite emerald-green blazer, she pulled them on quickly. Shoes, handbag, earrings, everything coordinated. Perfect.

But when she caught sight of her reflection in the mirror, a tired woman in her 30s stared back at her. Dark circles under her eyes, skin too pale, cheekbones too sharp. She looked drained.

A few swipes of makeup worked its magic, masking the exhaustion, smoothing over the stress. With a practiced hand, she covered the evidence of her sleepless nights, of the weight of responsibility pressing down on her.

6:45 AM.

Time to go. She grabbed her coffee in the kitchen. She felt the warmth in her cold hands. She took the first sip. Liquid gold. Smooth, strong, with just the right amount of bitterness to jolt her system into action. It was the only thing that kept her upright when exhaustion threatened to pull her under.

Caffeine, don't fail me now, she muttered as she stepped into the freezing morning, braced herself against the ice-cold wind, and marched into the battlefield.

Monday had begun.

2

THE DRAGONS' DEN

By the time Maya pulled into the office parking lot, her nerves were already frayed. The snowstorm had turned her commute into a white-knuckled test of patience, bumper-to-bumper traffic, brake lights flashing like warning signals, and near misses with drivers who apparently thought the road was theirs.

She sat in her car, gripping the steering wheel, her knuckles white, breathing through the tension still coiled tight in her chest. The world outside was a blur of frost and swirling snow, but inside, it was just her and the dull pounding of anxiety against her ribs.

Then her phone shattered the silence, its shrill ring jolting her. She fumbled for it, nearly dropping it in her lap. It was Andrea. Her assistant. The moment she answered, Andrea's voice came tumbling through, breathless and high-pitched.

"Oh, thank God you picked up! The weather is a nightmare. I was worried you weren't going to make it! The board members are already all here. Are you ready?"

Maya closed her eyes for a second, gathering herself.

"Good morning, Andrea," she said evenly. "And yes, I know what day it is."

"Good. Because everything depends on this presentation, Maya. If you don't nail it, our division..."

A sharp inhale. "We're all counting on you. Good luck!" The line went dead.

Dammit! Maya let out a slow breath, staring at the screen.

This day is already trying to kill me, she muttered under her breath.

She grabbed her half-empty coffee cup, shoved the car door open, and stepped into the freezing wind. The cold bit through her blazer instantly, sending a violent shiver down her spine. Snowflakes clung to her hair and shoulders as she hurried across the slick pavement, her heels clicking with urgency.

Inside, the office lobby was eerily quiet, and the hum of the heating system struggled against winter's grip. Overhead lights cast a sterile glow on tired faces, early arrivals trudging through their Monday morning rituals like ghosts in a gray-tinted world. Around her, more coworkers shuffled in, some with scarves wrapped tightly around their necks as if trying to shield themselves from reality. The office on a Monday morning was a universal experience: silent nods, slow blinks, the collective sigh of people who had already lost the battle with their inboxes.

First stop: More coffee. Maya moved toward the machine as if it were a lifeline, refilling her cup with shaky hands. The rich, familiar aroma swirled up, wrapping around her like a temporary comfort. She inhaled deeply, willing the caffeine to work its magic, to give her the energy she so desperately needed.

8

"Morning." The unexpected voice made her turn. Adam from finance stood beside her, hands tucked into his pockets. He was new and quiet. The kind of guy who seemed genuinely nice. Maya mustered a small smile, but she wasn't in the mood for small talk. Not today.

"Morning," she replied, her voice polite but distant. Adam nodded, as if sensing the walls she'd just put up, and stepped aside. She took one more sip of the bitter coffee, squared her shoulders, and made her way to the boardroom, where freezing temperatures were awaiting her. The scent of burnt coffee clung to the air, mixing with the nervous energy buzzing in her chest.

Then she heard it. A hush. A momentary stillness. And then ...his voice right beside her.

"Morning, Maya. You'd better show your best performance today."

It was Richard, her boss. His words were clipped, edged with that razor-sharp authority that had crushed many before her. His eyes bore into her, scanning for weakness like a predator locking onto its prey. His face was flushed, and his blood pressure always seemed one argument away from catastrophe.

Maya inhaled sharply, her fingers tightening around her laptop and presentation folder. This was it. The moment she had prepped for, rehearsed in the mirror for, willed herself to believe she was ready for. But standing under Richard's suffocating scrutiny, her confidence withered like a flower under a scorching sun.

She forced a smile. "Good morning, Richard! I ...uh ... I prepared my presentation."

His lips twisted into something between a smirk and a sneer. "You'd better."

9

And just like that, he was gone, sweeping past her and into the boardroom, leaving Maya frozen in place, her pulse hammering in her ears.

This wasn't just another presentation. This was survival.

Another sip of coffee. Her grip on her laptop tightened. Maya inhaled deeply, forcing air into her lungs as if she could steady herself with breath alone. Then, with every ounce of courage she could summon, she pushed open the massive wooden boardroom door that Richard just rushed through two seconds before her.

It was showtime, and Maya needed to be ready for it. She pulled all her strength together for that very moment she had been working so hard for.

Inside, a long, extravagant table stretched before her, lined with seven men in tailored suits sitting in a perfect row, their polished shoes and crisp suits exuding power. She felt small, and her crisp white shirt, black trousers, and her favorite emerald-green blazer suddenly seemed to not be the right choice for today. Richard was among the board members, making small talk, his deep voice blending seamlessly into the authoritative hum of the room.

No one acknowledged her. She moved swiftly to the corner, keeping her presence as small as possible, like a mouse scurrying along the edges of a room full of predators. First things first, connect the laptop.

Please, don't let the tech fail me, she thought to herself. She plugged in the computer. Found the remote for the screen. Stared at it.

Damn it. So many buttons. Which one? Her heart hammered. She glanced at her watch.

7:55. Five minutes before she was supposed to start. Her

hands were trembling. A wave of heat crashed over her, followed by an icy chill. Her pulse thundered in her ears.

And then ... A voice. Loud. Sharp.

"Good morning, Maya. Having trouble?"

The board assistant, Anita, had entered. Her tone cut through the thick silence like a blade. Maya's stomach twisted. Every single head in the room turned toward her. The air shifted, heavy with judgment. Richard's eyes darkened. He looked livid. Maya forced a smile, part relief, part resentment, as Anita took the remote from her shaking hand, pressed a few buttons, and like magic, the screen flickered to life.

"Here you go. You're all set! Good luck," Anita said, her voice too cheerful, too loud. Then she turned and left, the heavy door shut behind her.

There was no escape now. She was trapped in the dragon's den.

Maya stood in the center of the room, her back straight, but her insides twisted. Seven middle-aged men stared at her, their expressions unreadable, expecting her to deliver THE solution to years of unresolved organizational problems.

Thirty minutes. That's all she had.

She swallowed hard. "Good morning, everyone," she said, but her voice cracked.

A scoff. Then, a voice from the table: "Can't hear you. Speak up."

Maya steadied herself, gripping the edge of the table like an anchor.

"Good morning, everyone," she repeated, louder this time.

No smiles. No nods. Just blank, expectant faces.

She cleared her throat, pushing forward.

"Over the past months, our team has worked tirelessly to ..."

A hand waved at her, stopping her from continuing.

"Cut to the chase," the chairman interrupted, his voice as cold as the winter air outside.

"We don't need a recap of how hard you and your team worked. Let me remind you that it is your job. We need results. You have 25 minutes, Maya."

"Of course." She bit the inside of her cheek, willing herself to obey the rules. She felt how the sweat was pouring out of her pores into her not-so-crisp white shirt anymore. She pressed forward. Her voice grew steadier as she explained the scope of the issues, presenting months of painstaking research, laying the hard truth bare in front of the most powerful people in the corporation.

Just as she started regaining her confidence...

A strong voice silenced her. "I don't believe these numbers!" The Chief Finance Officer cut through her momentum like a knife. "This can't be right. How did you even come up with these figures?" She had spent days refining this, running numbers, ensuring every detail was airtight.

Maya met his stare. "I'd be happy to walk you through the detailed numbers later," she said, keeping her tone as calm as her voice permitted. Then, without waiting for permission, she moved on as quickly as possible in the hope her answer was sufficient to calm down the dragon.

Because now comes the hardest part.

She braced herself and presented the proposal. No easy fixes. No magic wands.

But as she spoke, she felt a subtle shift in energy.

Blank stares. Crossed arms. One man checked his watch. Another leaned back in his chair, unimpressed.

Then came the interruption.

"Maya, I see where you're going with this," said Mr. Reynolds, the Vice President. Diplomatic, but dismissive. "But I don't think this is the right direction for us."

Her stomach dropped.

"We need something... bolder," another board member chimed in. "More aggressive. This feels a little safe."

Safe? She had crunched these numbers to prove this was the smartest path forward. The best way to minimize risk while maximizing growth. But no ... what they wanted was something flashy. She opened her mouth to defend her work, but the discussion had already moved on, as if she had never spoken.

She clenched her jaw, nodding politely, pretending this didn't feel like a punch to the gut. As the meeting dragged on, she sat there, listening to them tear apart her strategy, her hard work, as if it were nothing. Then she heard the loud voice, "Thank you, Maya. That will be all. You can leave now."

She blinked. She stood frozen, her breath caught in her throat. They were dismissing her without any concrete answer. Outside this room, an entire division was waiting for answers. They were counting on her to walk out of here with a future.

And yet ...

Maya couldn't find the courage to argue. To demand to stay. To fight for her seat at this table. She swallowed hard.

"Thank you," she mumbled, her voice barely audible. She gathered her laptop, her papers, her pride, what was left of it, and walked out.

Maya barely registered the sound of chairs scraping as the executives moved on to the next item on the agenda. Her boss didn't look at her as he gathered his papers. No feedback. No reassurance. Just a dismissive glance before turning away.

Her heels clicked against the polished floor as she walked out, her pulse still pounding. The massive wooden door clicked shut behind her. She leaned against the wall, her breath shallow, her world tilting.

"At least I made it out of the dragon's den alive today. But how long can I keep doing this?"

3

ASHES AND APPLAUSE

The meeting had been an unmitigated disaster. Maya had walked into the boardroom prepared, or so she thought. She had rehearsed her points, refined her data, and braced herself for the inevitable push-back. But the moment she started speaking, the room shifted. The expressions had tightened, the murmurs of side conversations stopped, and then the real interrogation began.

"Did you even consider the long-term risk?" she still heard the Vice President's voice echoing in her head. The question had been fired like a gunshot, cutting through her presentation. She had opened her mouth to respond, but the words got tangled in her throat. The numbers were there. The strategy was sound, wasn't it?

She had looked toward her boss Richard several times during her 30 minutes of hell, hoping for a nod, a lifeline ... anything. Instead, he leaned back in his chair, arms crossed, the weight of his silence more damning than words. She had hoped for help in this situation. Not today. Not from Richard. Was this too much to ask for?

Every misstep, every hesitation, had fueled the storm. The board's skepticism thickened the air. Questions were fired at her faster than she could deflect them. She wasn't even sure anymore if she had been presenting a strategy or just defending herself from an onslaught of doubt.

She had not nailed it.

She had crashed and burned.

Andrea was waiting around the corner. Normally, her assistant's face was a mix of quiet admiration and unwavering efficiency. But today? Today, she looked hesitant. That alone was confirmation enough.

"Tough room," Andrea said finally, handing Maya a bottle of water.

"Board wasn't exactly... thrilled. I heard from Anita."

Anita. That meant her failure was already circulating.

Maya took the water, but it felt heavy in her hands. Her throat was dry, her skin hot. The familiar pang of failure settled deep in her stomach. She hated this feeling. Hated the way it gnawed at her, the way it made her feel like she was slipping. And yet, lately, that sensation had been creeping in more often, like a slow, inevitable leak in a ship she wasn't sure how to patch.

"They want a follow-up strategy by the end of the day," Andrea continued carefully.

"PR also needs a statement about your award. Oh, and marketing is asking if you could post something about it." Maya let out a sharp breath.

"Right. The award."

The award was created over a decade ago to spotlight outstanding female leaders, trailblazers who broke ceilings, built legacies, and inspired others to do the same. A framed badge of honor. A symbol of excellence. Andrea had recommended her for it. Well, pushed her.

"You're a perfect candidate," she'd said. Maya had completed the application between meetings and midnight emails, barely remembering what she wrote, never expecting to win. And now, the irony: a leadership award landing on the same day she had watched her credibility shrink in the eyes of the people who mattered most in this corporation.

Andrea read her mind and hesitated.

"Do you want me to draft the statement?" Maya nodded.

"Make it sound... inspiring. 'Honored and grateful' all that."

She tried to muster a smile, but it barely reached her lips.

"Thank you, Andrea."

Before Andrea could say anything else, Maya turned and walked straight to her office, avoiding eye contact with anyone along the way. She didn't feel like talking. Not now. Maybe not for the rest of the day.

The moment she sat at her desk, Maya let out a slow exhale and pressed her fingers to her temples.

A deep breath. Then another.

She unlocked her phone, and the notifications continued to pour in.

LinkedIn was overflowing with congratulatory messages.

"A true leader."

"An inspiration."

"Your work ethic is unmatched."

A notification from *Business Insider* caught her eye. The winners had just been announced. Her name was there, displayed in bold letters under *Top Women in Business.* Her fingers tightened around her phone. On Instagram, her latest post, a carefully curated black-and-white head shot, chin lifted, gaze sharp, was exploding with likes and comments. *#BossMoves #WomenInLeadership #Trailblazer.* Colleagues tagging her in posts, singing her praises:

"So honored to work with the incredible Maya Sinclair!"

"A powerhouse in the Corporate world!"

Her inbox now started to become a jungle of PR requests, interview invitations, and partnership offers, among all the internal demands.

From the outside, she was unstoppable.

From the inside? She felt like a fraud.

She scrolled through the flood of admiration, feeling an odd sense of detachment. Every glowing comment, every polished headline, was like a thin layer of gold paint over something cracking underneath.

If only they knew.

If only they knew that she had barely slept in weeks.

That she had been drowning in unread emails, botched meetings, and the creeping sense that she wasn't enough. That she was failing in the very rooms where she had spent years proving herself.

Her world was crumbling, but online?

Online, she was *untouchable.*

Maya let her phone drop onto the desk and leaned back in her chair, staring at the ceiling.

She had built an empire on the perception of strength. But today, for the first time, she wondered how much longer she could hold it all together.

Something had to change.

"I can't do this anymore!"

4

DROWNING

Maya stared at the screen. Her inbox was still an abyss of unanswered emails. Her calendar held her tight with back-to-back meetings. During the day, faces flickered in and out of her screen, voices droning on in online meetings, but she was barely present. The irony was sharp, surrounded by people, yet utterly alone. A ghost haunting her own career.

By the time her clock hit 5:00 PM, something inside her shifted. For the first time in weeks - months, maybe - she felt the day was over. Normally, she was the last to leave, turning off the lights, ensuring the battlefield was cleared for another war tomorrow.

As she passed her assistant's desk, a look of surprise crossed Andrea's face.

"You are leaving? Already? But..." Andrea surprisingly said. "I sent you the PR statement for the awards. The PR team is pressing to release it." Maya barely heard her. Her body felt like it was moving through water, heavy, sluggish, disconnected.

"I leave it with you," she muttered, the words tasting foreign, unnatural on her tongue. It wasn't like her to let go. "Send it out."

Andrea blinked. "And Richard is still expecting the follow-up strategy by tonight."

There it was. The final punch. A wave of nausea rolled through Maya, her vision darkening at the edges. Richard. Always Richard. Demanding, relentless, impossible.

"He'll have to wait." Her voice was sharper than she intended, but she didn't care. She turned on her heels and rushed out of the building, leaving Andrea in stunned silence.

The cold evening air hit her like a slap. She gasped, and suddenly, the dam inside her broke. Tears poured out, unbidden, unstoppable. She wasn't crying. She was leaking, hemorrhaging weeks, months, maybe years of suppressed exhaustion.

Her feet barely remembered the way to her car. She collapsed into the driver's seat, gripping the wheel like an anchor. Her sobs were silent at first, but then they came in waves - deep, guttural, gasping. The kind of crying that steals your breath, that makes your chest ache like a wound ripped open.

What had happened? Where was this bright, ambitious, impervious Maya?

By the time she started the car, she couldn't remember how long she had sat there. The drive home was a blur, just an endless stretch of lights and turns; she barely registered. She was on autopilot, guiding her through a life she no longer recognized.

When she reached her apartment, she didn't turn on the lights. Didn't bother with dinner. Instead, she wrapped herself in a blanket, curled up on the couch, and flicked through the TV channels, watching meaningless faces and hearing meaningless words.

She needed something stronger. Something to drown the today's negative moments which haunted her, and to blur the sharp edges of loneliness clawing at her chest. Something to replace the gnawing sense of failure, the voice in her head whispering that she was a fraud, an imposter, a woman decorated with awards she didn't deserve.

Wine. That would help. Or vodka. Maybe both? Something strong enough to wipe out reality and replace it with a temporary illusion. A version of herself that didn't care, didn't hurt, didn't feel so damned alone and helpless.

She rummaged through the kitchen like a woman on a mission, finding victoriously a bottle of red wine from France. Merlot. Elegant. Sophisticated. A drink for someone in control. A laugh nearly escaped her lips. Tonight, she would pair her regrets with this nice bottle of wine. She poured a large glass.

And just as the warmth of the alcohol began to take the sting out of her emptiness, just as her mind started to soften under the influence, she ruined it all by picking up her phone out of habit, scrolling mindlessly on social media. There, on her screen, was a polished image of her, poised, confident, radiant. The announcement of her Exceptional Leadership Award was everywhere, accompanied by congratulatory comments, praise, and admiration. Her stomach twisted. She took another big sip of her Merlot in the hope of drowning the negative feelings arising.

Who was this woman? This version of herself, airbrushed and untouchable, looking back at her with a dazzling smile? It felt like she was staring at a stranger.

A laugh bubbled up inside her - cold, bitter. Was this woman the same one drowning on her couch, feeling like her own life was suffocating her? The disconnect was unbearable.

Her phone buzzed. Richard. Again. She took another sip of Merlot in desperation and decided to ignore the phone. She turned it face down. She couldn't bear another lecture. The weight of expectations pressed against her chest. She was a machine to them - always producing, always performing, always available. But no one asked how she felt. Not Richard. Not her colleagues. Not the dozens of congratulatory messages flooding her inbox, celebrating a success that felt like a cruel joke.

She wasn't a machine. She was human. A woman on the edge, desperate for air, for silence, for something real.

Eventually, exhaustion and perhaps a generous dose of Merlot took over. She drifted into sleep right there on the couch, tangled in blankets, surrounded by the hum of the TV and the distant sounds of the city.

Outside, life continued.

But Maya?

Maya was drowning.

"Maybe I need to disappear ...

just for a little while," she thought.

5

AFTERMATH

Maya woke up late, but for the first time in forever, she didn't scramble out of bed. Or, well, off the couch. She groaned, peeling her eyes open only to be greeted by a stabbing headache that made her regret every single sip of Merlot she had had last night.

The TV was still on, playing some mindless morning show. An empty wine bottle lay on the floor beside the couch, along with too many items scattered all over the apartment. A half-full glass (no, scratch that, half-empty, much like her soul), balanced precariously on the armrest.

She just lay there, staring at the ceiling. Her head throbbed. Her mouth was dry. Her phone on the table blinked. It looked like evidence from a crime scene.

The crime? Neglecting to be the perfect, reliable, high-achieving Maya that everyone expected.

She squinted at the clock on the wall. 9:07 AM. By now, she would usually be deep in emails, already on her third coffee, possibly fighting the urge to throw her laptop out the window.

Instead, she was here. In the silence. In the mess.

She groaned, rubbing her temples. What now?

As Maya sat upright on the couch, her skull nearly imploded. She took her phone. She stared at missed calls and unread messages. 5 calls from Richard (of course! Not because he cared, but because he wanted the follow-up strategy.), 3 calls from Andrea (poor, dedicated Andrea) and a never-ending flood of messages ranging from "URGENT" to "WHERE ARE YOU???" to a passive-aggressive "Hope everything's okay" that somehow felt more threatening than all the rest.

Panic surged in her chest, but for once, she didn't scramble. She didn't leap up, throw on a blazer, and attempt to salvage the day. She did not find the energy to do so. Instead, she did something else. Reckless. Borderline rebellious.

She dialed Andrea.

"Maya! Oh my god, Richard is..."

"I'm not coming to the office today," Maya said, cutting her off.

For a moment, there was absolute silence. In 10 years, Andrea had never seen Maya miss a single day. She always showed up. She was always there. Like a strong soldier holding up at the battlefront.

"...What?"

"I will take the day off. Call in sick. You know, headache, nausea, stomach cramps, and ... it seems like... a deep existential crisis."

Andrea hesitated, as if waiting for the punchline. "But Richard—"

"Richard will survive."

Andrea inhaled sharply, either in shock or admiration. Maybe both.

"Okay," she said, voice lowering. "Should I tell him you'll check emails later or …"

"No." Maya was caught by surprise by her direct answer.

Another pause.

"Should I tell him when you'll be back?"

"Undecided. Maybe never."

A strangled sound came from Andrea's end, possibly a suppressed laugh.

"Alright. I'll, uh, figure something out."

For once, the world could keep spinning without her.

Today, the battlefield will have to survive without its best soldier.

Maya hung up and collapsed back onto the couch, phone slipping from her fingers. The room spun slightly. Her head pounded. Her mouth tasted like regret. But despite the chaos, despite the mess, despite the storm that was undoubtedly brewing at the office without her, she felt something she hadn't in a long time.

Relief.

6

DIALING FOR ANSWERS

It could all wait, she told herself, just for a little while longer. Dragging herself to the kitchen, she grabbed an aspirin and a glass of water, swallowing both with the urgency of someone trying to erase the evidence of last night's poor decisions. Hunger gnawed at her stomach, so she poured herself a bowl of cereal. The milk sloshed over the edges as she moved in a daze.

A shower. That might help. Wash away the headache. The doubts. The heaviness pressing against her chest. Freshly showered, with damp hair clinging to her neck, she collapsed onto the couch again, legs curled underneath her. She was endlessly tired, and even the coffee did not help today. She needed... something. A sign? A life raft? Just someone to help her make sense of her struggle at work and her suffocating emptiness.

Her first instinct was Emma. Her dear sister had always been the one to ground her, the one who never made her feel unworthy. Maybe she could talk to her, unload some of this existential mess, and lift her up for a moment when she

27

desperately needed it.

She pressed call and waited.

One ring. Two.

Then chaos.

"MAAAX! PUT THAT DOWN!" she heard Emma screaming on the other end. A loud crash followed. It must have been a toy hitting the wall. Maya heard the indignant voice of her tiny nephew, "It wasn't me!" in the background.

Maya flinched, pulling the phone slightly away from her ear. "Uh, Emma?"

A sharp exhale. "Maya! Hey, sorry, hold on ...LUCAS, IF YOU THROW ONE MORE TOY,

I SWEAR..."

Maya heard muffled sounds of shuffling, running water, and something clattering

against a counter. Emma was in the trenches.

"Bad timing?" Maya asked, already knowing the answer.

Emma let out a breathless laugh.

"Is there ever a good time with two tiny humans demanding me 24/7?"

"Fair," Maya responded.

She hesitated, debating whether to actually open up or just let it slide.

But before she could decide, another voice whined in the background.

"Mom! I'm hungry!"

"Hold on, Maya," Emma said, voice muffled as she moved.

"Yes, darling, I'm making it—NO, YOU CANNOT EAT CEREAL OFF THE FLOOR!"

Maya exhaled slowly. "*Yeah. Not happening,*" she thought to herself, and said to Emma

"You know what? Never mind. Just checking in."

Emma barely had time to process that before the oven timer beeped.

"Crap, the muffins! Look, I gotta go. Are you OK?"

"Yeah," Maya lied.

"Great, love you! Talk to you over the weekend."

Click. She hung up.

Maya dropped the phone onto her stomach and stared at the ceiling again. She felt more than ever how the loneliness surrounded her. She fell into another state of trance, half-awake, half-asleep. The TV was murmuring in the background. At some point, she became aware of the sun shifting through her blinds. It was already noon.

She dragged herself off the couch and made herself a toast. It tasted like nothing to her today. Her fingers absently scrolled through social media while she ate. This was a terrible decision. Everyone looked so put together. So successful. Thriving. Like life had given them some secret manual she had somehow missed.

Then, there he was.

Ethan.

A picture of him, laughing at some rooftop bar, drink in hand, happy. The kind of happiness that shouldn't have made her stomach twist, but did anyway. Before she could stop herself, her thoughts went there. Wasn't this the moment people reached out to their ex-boyfriends? When they felt low and needed someone familiar to tell them they weren't a complete disaster? She stared at his name in her contact list. It had been so long. Would he even pick up? Her thumb hovered over the call button.

And just like that, the memory of that night surfaced. The

last time she had seen him. They had been at that little Italian place, the one with the dim lighting and overpriced wine. What started as a normal dinner had cracked something fundamental between them.

"You're never here, Maya," he had said, pushing his plate aside.

"That's ridiculous. I'm literally sitting in front of you."

He laughed. But not the good kind.

"You know what I mean. You're always working. Always checking your phone. It's like I'm competing with your job, and guess what? I'm losing."

She had rolled her eyes. "Ethan, I have responsibilities."

"And I don't?" His jaw had tightened. "I just wanted to matter too."

She had scoffed, actually scoffed, and said, "You don't understand ambition."

And that was it. The moment he shut down. The moment she knew it was over, even before he stood up and left.

Now, staring at his name on her screen, she felt that same weight in her chest. He had wanted her, not this overworked, stretched-thin version she had become. But she didn't know how to be another person anymore. With a sigh, she locked her phone. Calling Ethan wasn't the answer.

She fell back into her trance state in front of the TV. The hours went by without Maya noticing. By the afternoon, Maya felt restless. The apartment felt too quiet, like the silence itself was pressing against her chest.

So, naturally, she turned to the last person. The person who raised her knew her from the beginning and always had an opinion on her life. Her mom. A woman who had always held impossibly high expectations. Praise came rarely to her, only after perfection. Maya could still hear her voice from childhood:

"You're capable of more," even when she thought she was already giving it all.

She dialed.

"Maya!" her mother answered cheerfully.

"Calling me in the middle of the day? What's the occasion? Anything wrong with you?"

Maya exhaled. "I took the day off."

Silence. Heavy, uncomfortable silence.

"Are you sick?"

"Sort of."

A pause.

"What do you mean, 'sort of'?"

"Mom, I'm just tired."

Then came the classic Mom sigh. "Sweetheart, you can't just stay home because you're

tired. Everyone gets tired. You push through it!"

Maya rubbed her temples. "I don't think it's that simple, Mom."

"Of course it is. You're doing amazing at work! You got a promotion recently. You need the

money to survive in the city. And I saw you got that award. What was it for? Exceptional

Leadership? See? You're fine!"

Fine?

Maya didn't feel fine.

"Maya, listen to me," her mother continued. "Have some coffee, get some fresh air, and

go back to the office tomorrow. You've worked too hard to throw it all overboard

because of... whatever this is."

Maya closed her eyes. "Okay, Mom."

"That's my girl. Now, I have to run. Meeting some friends for dinner. Love you!"

The line went dead.

Maya sat on the couch with her phone still in her hand. She pulled the blanket around her shoulders. Her stomach was churning, and her head was pounding while the TV was broadcasting the latest news, and the buzz of the city outside continued.

Emma was too busy.

Ethan was gone.

Mom didn't understand.

No one was actually listening.

She had spent the entire day searching for someone to tell her what to do, how to fix this.

But maybe no one out there could.

Maybe she had to figure it out herself.

II

TIME OUT

*"The wound is the place
where the light enters you."*
Rumi

7

ONE CLICK AWAY

The next day, Maya woke up late. Again.

The moment she opened her eyes, a familiar jolt of panic shot through her. Work. She should be checking emails. Following up. Working on the Follow-up Strategy. Making sure Richard wasn't on the verge of having a meltdown. She reached for her phone, already dreading the flood of messages waiting for her - seven missed calls from Richard, four from Andrea, and 73 new unread emails.

She groaned and stared at the screen without reading anything. Her brain screamed at her. You can't just ignore this! You have responsibilities. You are the one people count on. And yet, she couldn't bring herself to care. Normally, she would have already been on her second dose of caffeine, answering emails, fighting fires, proving (for the millionth time) that she was resilient, capable, reliable, essential. Instead, she just sat there, without any energy, wrapped in a blanket, staring at the screen of her untouched laptop. If she opened it, the weight of everything would come crashing down. The pending strategy documents. The PR fallout. The endless threads of urgent, high-priority tasks that had never actually felt urgent until someone else decided they were.

Her stomach twisted. She knew she should be working. But for the first time in her life, she didn't care. And that terrified her. She needed something - anything - to pull her out of this feeling.

Grabbing her phone again, she mindlessly scrolled through social media. She told herself it was just for a minute. A distraction. A small break before she faced reality. But instead of a break, she found something else.

It appeared like a miracle in her feed. Pictures of a distant island, golden beaches stretching into endless turquoise water. Palm trees swaying in the breeze. A small wooden lodge, perched right by the ocean, sunlight spilling onto its terrace.

Disconnect. Recharge. Escape. It said.

Maya stared at the social media post.

God, how ridiculous. She thought.

She scrolled past it.

But then, after a second, she scrolled back.

She stared at the picture for a moment, imagining her sitting on that very beach, her feet in the sand surrounded by palm trees with the sun glazing over her.

She snapped out of her dream. This was absurd. She couldn't just leave. She had too much work. She couldn't afford it. And yet...

Wasn't work the reason she felt so miserable in the first place? She needed a timeout. She closed her eyes, pressing her fingertips against her forehead. She could almost hear Richard's voice, the inevitable conversation if she dared to leave now.

You're taking time off? Now? With everything happening?
Maya, you know you're the only one who can handle this.
Just push through. We need you.

And the worst part? He'd be right.

Because Maya had built her entire identity around her work. Her being the person who never lets anything slip. The one who handled things. The one who never needed a break. But she wasn't handling things. She was drowning.

And this beach?

Was it to escape reality?

Was it an answer?

A way to stop this endless cycle before she collapsed completely?

Her pulse quickened as she clicked the link for more information. One click led to another. Soon, she was deep in a website filled with photos of paradise—clear blue waters, untouched beaches, hammocks swaying lazily under palm trees on a remote island. No resorts. No overbooked tourist attractions. Just a quiet, forgotten corner of the world where no one would expect her to answer emails. There was even a section for accommodations: small, rustic beach lodges. No luxury. No distractions. Just the sound of the waves and the feeling of sand under her feet.

She imagined herself there again. Waking up to the ocean instead of a calendar full of meetings. Drinking coffee on a terrace instead of speed-walking to a conference call.

For the first time in forever, she felt something other than exhaustion.

She felt a glimpse of hope.

And that tiny flicker of hope, that whisper of *what if*, was all it took.

Her laptop still sat on the table, unopened. A symbol of everything she was supposed to be doing. Her work phone buzzed again. Another call. Another urgent request. She let it ring.

Her heartbeat quickened as she clicked through the booking page.

One lodge: only one more available.

One flight to paradise: leaving in two days.

She hesitated.

The price flashed on the screen.

It wasn't outrageous. But it wasn't cheap either. Especially not now. Maya barely makes it through the month till she gets paid again. She had a good job, but the cost of living had skyrocketed in the past years without her paycheck being raised at the same speed, even though she got a promotion. She hadn't even checked her credit card balance in a week because she was afraid of what it might say after fixing her car the other day. Some distant voice was telling her: *You should be more responsible. You can't afford an extravagant vacation right now.*

She stared at the numbers for a moment. This was the price of her escape.

On the other hand, she thought, *what would be the price for staying home and continuing the way she did right now?*

What was the price of losing herself more and more, every single day?

Of waking up in panic, of falling asleep in dread?

Of pretending to be okay, when your soul has long gone silent?

How much was that life costing her?

And how long could she keep paying for it?

She closed her eyes for a moment and drew in a shaky breath.

Then, without giving herself time to reconsider, she filled out the information and booked it in the hopes the credit card would still take in the amount. And it did.

Flight confirmed.

Lodge reserved.

Maya stared at the confirmation email, her hands slightly trembling.

Had she really just done that?

She had.

And the most shocking part?

For the first time in months, she felt real excitement.

Not knowing yet that the next week would change her life forever.

8

CONFESSION

The next day, Maya woke up with a jolt. For a moment, disoriented. The events of yesterday trickled back like slow, sticky honey. The email confirmation. The flight. The lodge.

Oh god. She had actually done it.

Her heart pounded as she reached for her phone, as if expecting reality to have erased her impulsive decision overnight. But no! There it was, sitting smugly in her inbox: Flight confirmed. Departure in one day. A knot formed in her stomach.

What the hell have I done?

She had never done something so reckless. So irresponsible. She had built an entire career on calculated risks, on always having a backup plan, an emergency exit, a safety net. And now, she had thrown herself off the ledge without checking if there was water below!

Maya sat up, gripping the blanket around her shoulders. The warmth of the apartment suddenly felt suffocating. Her inbox, no doubt overflowing, called to her like a ticking bomb, demanding her attention.

Another notification popped up.

Richard: *Call me. Now.*

The second one, just as expected:

Andrea: *Maya, where ARE you?*

She groaned, rubbing her temples. Of course, they had noticed by now. Her absence was like a missing piece in the corporate machine. And Richard? He was going to explode when she will tell him about her escape.

She hesitated, thumb hovering over the call button, before finally taking a deep breath and pressing the dial. The line barely rang before he picked up.

"Where the hell have you been?" His voice was razor-sharp, each syllable laced with fury. "I've been calling you since yesterday. This isn't like you, Maya. Do you have any idea how bad this looks?" She swallowed. Her throat was dry. She pulled all her energy together for this one sentence.

"I ... I need a break."

Silence. The kind that made her stomach twist.

"A break?" Richard repeated, as if she had spoken in a foreign language.

"You think now is the time for a break?

Do you have any idea what you've just done?

Everyone is asking questions. The board is ..."

"I don't care about the board." The words slipped out before she could stop them.

Another silence, this one was more dangerous.

"Maya," Richard said slowly, as if speaking to a child.

"You *do* understand that walking away like this could cost you your career?"

Something inside her snapped. "Walking away? I haven't quit, Richard. I just ..."

She exhaled sharply. "I just need some time for myself."

"Time," he echoed flatly. "For what?"

For what? To breathe? To stop feeling like a machine? To remember what it was like to exist outside of endless deadlines and power plays at work?

But she knew none of those answers would satisfy him.

"I'll be back in ten days," she said instead, her voice steadier than she felt.

A sharp inhale on the other end.

"Unbelievable," he muttered. "You think you can just disappear and come back like nothing happened?"

"Yes," she said simply.

For the first time in years, she was choosing herself over the job.

There was a long pause before Richard spoke again. This time, his voice was icy.

"Fine. Take your break, Maya. But expect consequences when you return."

And then the line went dead.

Maya stared at the phone. Her heart was hammering. A strange mix of fear and relief washed over her. She was trembling. Was she making the biggest mistake of her life? Or was this the moment she finally set herself free?

Time will tell. For now, she had one more call to make.

Andrea, her assistant, picked up instantly.

"Oh my god, Maya, what is happening?" Andrea's voice was frantic, laced with genuine concern. "Richard is going nuclear. The board is whispering. Everyone is asking where you are."

Maya exhaled, leaning against the kitchen counter. "I'm leaving."

"Leaving as in ... quitting?"

"No," she clarified. "Leaving as in disappearing for ten days."

A pause. Then, in a much quieter voice, Andrea asked, "Are you okay?"

The question caught her off guard.

For months, people had thrown accolades at her, demanded results, and expected miracles. No one had asked that.

Maya swallowed past the lump in her throat. "I don't know," she admitted.

Andrea let out a breath. "Maya, I have never seen you take a day off. Not once. If you need this, then screw them."

A small, broken laugh escaped Maya. "Thanks, Andrea."

Maya was ready to pack her luggage and leave the chaos behind.

One day until departure.

No turning back now.

She made the decision.

This was only the beginning. The beginning of a strong current that will carry her somewhere she had never dreamt of.

9

READY FOR TAKEOFF

This was it. The day. The point of no return.

Maya sat on her couch, her suitcase packed and standing proudly by the door like a silent accomplice to her escape. The excitement should have been buzzing through her veins, but instead, a nervous energy coiled tight in her stomach. She glanced around her apartment, her kingdom of chaos.

The empty wine bottle from three nights ago still lay on the floor, a relic of her last existential crisis. Papers were stacked in hazardous towers on her desk, laundry sat in an accusing pile, and the dirty dishes in the sink had started to form what looked suspiciously like a civilization of their own.

I should clean up... she thought, before immediately dismissing the idea.

No. She was leaving this mess behind. Future Maya, whoever she would be after eight days in paradise, can deal with it.

Her phone buzzed. A single notification. The taxi has arrived. Her heart did a little flip.

Too late to fix anything now. It all just has to wait.

Dragging her suitcase behind her, she made her way down-stairs, each step making the reality of her decision more solid. The moment she stepped outside, she was hit with a gust of cold wind that made her shiver. Winter is still keeping its icy fingers wrapped around the city, and everyone moved through the streets like joyless, overworked ghosts.

The taxi was idling at the curb, blocking traffic. A chorus of honking erupted behind it as impatient drivers lost their minds.

Maya rushed forward, suddenly feeling like a fugitive escaping the scene of a crime.

"Good morning," she mumbled as she climbed in, breathless. "Thanks for waiting."

The driver didn't even acknowledge her. Not a nod. Not a grunt. Just a blank stare at the road before peeling away from the curb.

Wow. Someone woke up and chose rudeness. She buckled up and turned to stare out the window as the city blurred past. The grey buildings, the grim faces of early commuters, the suffocating familiarity of it all. It suddenly felt like another world. One she no longer belonged to.

The taxi passed her usual spots. The supermarket where she bought the same groceries on autopilot every week. The coffee shop where she had inhaled espresso shots like oxygen. The cinema, *when was the last time I even went to a movie?*

They hit a red light, right outside her office. The massive tower loomed over her, a glass-and-steel monument to stress. The oversized company logo sat smugly on the front, its bold letters practically sneering at her.

Inside, she could picture it all so clearly. The stiff suits moving from one meeting to another, eyes glued to screens, their souls slowly withering under fluorescent lights. Richard,

45

no doubt, was already terrorizing the team, barking orders and blaming her absence for all the world's problems. And Andrea, poor, sweet Andrea, was probably holding the fort, trying to keep everything from catching fire. Maya swallowed the guilt that rose in her throat. They would talk about her. No doubt. There would be whispers in the break room, raised eyebrows, and passive-aggressive comments.

Did you hear? Maya just... left.

Maybe she had a breakdown?

Leaving? In this situation. How irresponsible of her.

Went on vacation? Just like that? Unbelievable.

Her image was always important to her. She wanted to be that successful figure in the corporation that everybody adored. And with the years, it became even more important to her what people thought about her than what she thought about herself.

A honk jolted her out of her thoughts. The light had turned green. The taxi jerked forward, taking her further away from it all. She exhaled, sinking deeper into her seat. Suddenly, a nagging thought wormed its way into her mind. Shouldn't someone know where she was going? What if something happened? Her mother? No. That would be a disaster. Instead, she quickly typed out a message. MOM: *On vacation for seven days. Love you. Maya.*

She barely waited for a response before dialing the number of someone else who would actually understand her situation. Gina. The call barely rang twice before her best friend picked up.

"Alright, what's the emergency? You never call at this hour."

Maya took a breath. Then, without hesitation:

"I booked a flight to a remote island."

A beat of silence.

"You *what?!*"

A bubble of laughter escaped Maya's lips. A real one. The kind of laughter kids have when they do something forbidden. The kind she hadn't felt in months.

"Did I hit my head? Am I in an alternate universe? Maya Sinclair, the queen of spreadsheets and life plans, just booked a *spontaneous* trip?" Gina sounded like she had just witnessed a cat tap dance.

"I know," Maya admitted. "It's insane."

"It's iconic," Gina corrected. "And about damn time."

Maya exhaled, a small, nervous smile tugging at her lips. "I think I'm terrified."

"You should be," Gina teased. "You're about to do something real for once. No reports. No deadlines. Just you and... the unknown."

Maya chewed her lip. "Yeah."

"And let's be honest," Gina added, "you'd rather swim with real sharks than face your boss, Richard, right now."

Maya snorted. "You're not wrong."

Gina sighed dramatically.

"I love this for you! Go! Find yourself! Don't open the laptop. Don't look at your emails. Best to turn off WI-Fi. Meditate under a palm tree. Have a fling with a mysterious stranger. Drink some good cocktails for me. Have fun!"

Maya laughed again, lighter now.

"Thanks, Gina."

"Well, you better come back as a completely different person. It's about time you take a vacation just for you! You look like a ghost lately. Too thin, pale skin, and dark circles under your eyes." Gina said, mock-serious.

"I'm expecting enlightenment, glow-up energy, the whole

47

package."

Maya hesitated. "Different person, huh?"

But before she could unpack that, the taxi driver waved at her in the rear-view mirror, signaling they had arrived.

"Oh, crap Gina, I gotta go. Arrived at the airport. Boarding soon."

"Make the most out of it! Don't die." Gina said cheerfully.

"I'll try my best! Bye!"

Maya hung up and scrambled to gather her things.

As she stepped out of the car, and was immediately swallowed by the rush of the airport. People zigzagged around her, rolling suitcases clattering, voices rising and falling in a hundred different languages. A massive departure board loomed overhead, filled with endless destinations, when she entered the main hallway.

She scanned the screen, her heart hammering.

There it was. Flight 762—Departure: 10:30 AM—Destination: "Paradise".

Her fingers tightened around her suitcase handle.

Her pulse thrummed in her ears.

The doubt, the fear, the what-ifs, they all clawed at the edges of her mind.

The unknown was terrifying.

But maybe, just maybe, it was exactly what she needed.

10

THE LIMBO

The airport was a strange in-between place, a limbo of sorts. A place where people hovered between where they had been and where they were going. A place of transition, of restless energy, of hurried goodbyes and hopeful new beginnings. And now, Maya was just another lost soul in this sea of departures.

The line at check-in stretched endlessly, filled with people clutching their passports like golden tickets to freedom. Couples, families, and solo travelers are all waiting for their escape. She was just one of them. One of many who wanted to leave something behind.

As she stepped forward inch by inch, her grip on her bag tightened. Her heart pounded not from excitement, but from something she couldn't quite name. Was it guilt? Fear? The gnawing thought that this was a mistake?

"Next!" The airline agent barely looked at her, processing her documents with mechanical efficiency. For him, Maya was just another passenger, just another ticket to be processed. But for Maya, this wasn't just a ticket, it was proof. Proof that she was leaving. Proof that she made a decision and is now actually going forward with it. As she held the boarding pass in her hands, she felt its weight. This was it. No turning back now.

The security check line was long. It moved very slowly. Passengers got impatient. Maya always dreaded it. She did not like to be screened from top to bottom. What if they find something wrong, and she has to turn back? If getting out of her old life was this complicated, no wonder she had stayed stuck for so long.

Finally, she made it and pulled off her jacket, placing her bag on the conveyor belt. The X-ray machine hummed, scanning every inch of her belongings. Her laptop, her phone, her neatly packed toiletries, everything exposed under the harsh glare of security.

"Step forward," the officer commanded.

She took a breath and walked through the scanner.

BEEP. Maya's stomach dropped.

"Step back, please," the officer said harshly, expression unreadable.

"Shoes off. Belt, earrings. Any coins in your pocket?"

"No, Sir," she mumbled, fumbling to remove everything that could possibly betray her.

As she stepped through again … nothing. Silence. Relief flooded her. She scooped up her belongings, stuffing her feet back into her shoes, hands shaking slightly as she grabbed her bag. Why was she so nervous? She wasn't smuggling anything. She wasn't a fugitive. And yet, she felt like one.

One last obstacle. Passport control. The border officer took her passport with slow, deliberate hands, flipping through the pages. He stared at the screen, brows furrowing slightly. Maya held her breath.

Did he see it?

Did he somehow know she was running away from her life?

Did the system flag her as a woman on the verge of abandoning everything?

She swallowed hard, inwardly pleading: Just let me go!

The officer glanced at her. And then THUMP. The heavy stamp landed on the page. A crisp mark of approval. A visual confirmation that she was officially leaving. She exhaled. The past was behind her now. At least for some days. The reality of her office. The suffocating inbox. The meetings. The expectations. Even herself, the version of Maya that had felt trapped, small, and exhausted. She had been wanting to leave it behind so desperately.

She had no idea what lay ahead. No idea what this trip would bring. But she knew one thing. She didn't want what she had left behind. She was ready for the unknown. For a new beginning, only she could shape. The thought sent a thrill of excitement through her, but also fear. She had never traveled alone before, never ventured somewhere so unfamiliar, so disconnected. No Ethan to take care of the logistics. No one to reassure her when things went wrong. Just her. And that terrified her.

The waiting area at her gate buzzed with the sounds of other travelers, conversations in different languages, the crinkle of snack wrappers, and the hum of the overhead announcements. She found a seat in the middle of it. She was already exhausted by the morning. She gazed out of the window. On the horizon, she saw the city she would leave behind for a week. The city she grew up in. The city where she learned to walk, where she found her first love, and where she landed her first job. The city that shaped her. The city she has always adored. As beautiful as the skyline was from this window, somehow it did not feel right for her anymore.

She lived in that city and had a job. A "dream job" many would call. The title sounds impressive. She liked the work she was doing and collaborating with her assistant Andrea and the whole team was just fine, but her boss was scrutinizing her. Richard kept her small. And the board members? She was always crawling, not walking. Always aware of every single step she was taking, looking out for landmines. Her wings have been clipped.

Working so hard has let her forget about the joy of city life. When was the last time she went to the movies with her friends? She used to love to do that when she was younger. She could not even remember it. When was the last time she went out for a nice dinner? Oh, that was with Ethan, her ex-boyfriend. And it did not end well. She felt lonely in the ocean of a million people. Ethan was gone. And her hopes to find another boyfriend soon in her current situation are below zero. Honestly, she did not even have time lately to keep up with her closest friends or even her family. Not even to get out and do some sports. She used to belong to a running club, where she would do a group run of at least 10 kilometers every Sunday. It was not only the sports she enjoyed, but also the conversations she had along the way. No matter what weather - sun, snow, rain, storms - she would run. What had happened? She remembered. At one point, she got a promotion with new, greater responsibilities. She wanted to deliver and prove she was the right fit for the job. She started working harder, and by the end of the week, she was exhausted. She could not find the energy to get up from her couch. Instead, she preferred to stay home and zap through the TV and scroll through social media to get her dopamine fix. Besides, life in the city got expensive, and going out was a luxury she could not afford. That was her current reality in this city that she was about to leave behind.

The final boarding call flashed on the screen. It was time. Maya stepped forward, handing over her ticket and passport for one final check. She hesitated. Even though she knew from the bottom of her heart this was right for her, she was terrified to step into the unknown.

Could she still back out?

Could she turn around, go home, and pretend she had never booked this ticket?

"Have a good flight," the attendant said with a warm smile, handing back her documents.

She swallowed. Her feet refused to move.

"Excuse me," a voice muttered behind her, irritated. "Some of us have planes to catch."

Maya blinked, snapping out of her frozen moment, and took the step forward.

The grey boarding tunnel stretched ahead of her, swallowing her whole. She was moving.

The aircraft cabin smelled of coffee and recycled air. She found her seat by the window, tucking herself into the small space like she could somehow make herself disappear. She curled into her seat, instinctively searching for the comfort she would normally find on her couch under a pile of blankets. But there was no comfort here. Just a stiff seat, limited legroom, and a sky that stretched endlessly beyond the window. Outside, the world was grey, the cold wind leaving ice crystals on the glass. She watched as the baggage carts rolled past below her. She saw her suitcase being lifted into the belly of the plane. The only familiar piece, which left the city with her.

Passengers settled in around her. People stored their bags, flipped through magazines, and adjusted their seats. Some looked excited, others impatient. Some, like her, were simply lost in thought.

The cabin crew started their security instructions. "In case of emergency ..." she heard. *What if I were to die in an airplane crash now?* She thought. *What a horrible thought!* For a moment, she was terrified by the fact of dying. At one point, we all die, but Maya decided this was not the right time for it. She didn't want to leave Earth like that. She still had things to do. She knew there was more to life than what she had been experiencing. And she was ready to find it.

Then, exhaustion hit. A heavy, undeniable weight pressed her down. The whirlwind of emotions, the stress of the last few weeks, all came crashing down at once. Before the captain even welcomed them aboard, before she could overthink one more thing, her body surrendered, and Maya drifted into sleep.

She was leaving.

And when she woke up, she would be somewhere new.

Somewhere unknown.

Somewhere that might just change everything.

11

ARRIVAL

"Welcome! We have just landed. The local time is 4:00 PM, and it's a toasty 35 degrees Celsius. The rainy season is in full swing, and rain is what welcomes us today. Enjoy your stay nevertheless!"

Maya was jolted awake by the captain's voice, her mind struggling to catch up with reality. The chatter of passengers, the overhead compartments slamming shut, the rustling of bags being yanked from the overhead bins. It was all too loud, too chaotic. For a second, she was disoriented, caught between the haze of sleep and the stark realization that she had arrived.

The reality hit her. She was here.

The place she had booked on a whim, desperately seeking an escape. The place she had thrown herself toward without knowing if it was an escape or just another mistake.

A memory of Gina's voice echoed in her head: "I love this for you. Go! Find yourself. Don't open the laptop. Don't check your emails. Best to turn off WI-Fi. Meditate under a palm tree. Have a fling with a mysterious stranger. Drink good cocktails for me. And for the love of God, have fun!" Maya smirked. Despite her fear, she promised herself to try to do exactly what Gina told her.

With that thought in mind, she stood up, stretched her stiff limbs, and braced herself to step into the unknown.

The second she got off the plane, the hot air hit her thick, humid, and rich with the scent of spices and wet earth. It was like stepping into a wall of heat, an invisible force wrapping around her and making her instantly sticky. And then there was the rain. Not like the rain she was used to back home. It was strong, heavy, and relentless tropical rain.

She stood there for a second, blinking at the downpour, watching as passengers frantically unfolded raincoats and popped open umbrellas. She had neither. Within seconds, she was drenched just by walking from the airplane towards the airport hall. Her shirt clung to her like a second skin, water dripping from her hair, sliding down her spine. So much for arriving gracefully. She had envisioned stepping onto the island like some confident, independent traveler, looking effortlessly chic and composed. Instead, she looked like a drowned rat. Too late to turn back now.

She made her way toward the terminal, a structure with a thatched palm roof but no walls. It was just an open space, allowing the rain to mist through the air. Everything smelled earthy, fresh, and alive. People here looked different. Darker skin, shorter frames, bright, colorful clothes standing out against the stormy sky. Their movements were unhurried. No one was rushing, no one was complaining except for one loud tourist, a fellow passenger, who was yelling in English at a poor airport worker about the luggage delay. The worker merely smiled, nodded, and gestured vaguely. No urgency. No stress.

No answer to the question when?

Maya realizes she was a stranger in a strange place, she could not even speak the language. But maybe it was not strange. It was just new to her. After all, that is what she wanted.

Maya glanced around. She searched for a luggage belt. She couldn't find one. Instead, bags were being carried by hand from the airplane, slowly and methodically by the airport personnel, and dropped into a designated area on the wet ground.

It took ninety minutes till Maya finally spotted her suitcase. She exhaled in relief. She had only packed the essentials, but still, panic rose within her. What would she do without her luggage? No clothes, no toiletries, just a credit card and her phone? The thought alone made her stomach tighten. She wasn't that adventurous. Not yet, at least.

Dragging her soaked suitcase behind her, Maya spotted the rental car station, a small wooden stand with a handwritten sign reading CARS.

Another long wait. By the time she reached the front, she was exhausted, her wet clothes still clinging to her, and water was dripping onto the counter. The clerk, a small man with kind eyes, smiled warmly at her and asked in broken English,

"Where is your husband?"

Maya blinked. "Excuse me?"

"Your husband? He drives?"

Maya huffed out a breath, half amused, half irritated. "No husband. Just me."

The clerk's eyebrows shot up in surprise.

"Oh," he said, nodding slowly, like he needed a second to process the idea.

Maya rolled her eyes. As if a woman couldn't rent a car on

her own and drive it.

The next twenty minutes were a bureaucratic nightmare. Forms. More forms. Endless signing of things she barely skimmed … General Regulations, Insurance, Waiver Fees…. She was too tired to read all through the paperwork. Besides, the line of people behind her would not have appreciated her normally thorough revision, she would surely have done it back home. She would have questioned paragraphs and negotiated conditions. Not today. She surrendered. She could have been selling her soul for all she knew.

Finally, the clerk handed her a key and pointed toward the parking lot. She squinted through the rain and found no signs and no directions. The only thing she could see was a sea of cars. Alright, Maya. Let the treasure hunt begin.

Pressing the button on the key fob, she spotted a car blinking in the distance and ran toward it. She shoved her suitcase into the trunk and jumped inside, soaking her seat in the process. As she sat there, catching her breath, she reached for the steering wheel. It wasn't there. Her hands groped at nothing. She turned, slowly, and was horrified. The steering wheel was on the other side.

"Oh, you've got to be kidding me."

She groaned, dropping her forehead against the window. She hadn't even thought about this. That meant they drove on the other side of the road, too. She had never done that. She shuffled awkwardly into the driver's seat on the right-hand side. The real one this time.

"You got this, Maya!" She said to herself and stuck the key into the ignition.

The engine rumbled to life. Maya exhaled. *Okay. Not so bad.* Then she looked at the gear stick. And froze. It was manual.

She was only used to driving an automatic.

"Oh, come on!" She had never driven a stick shift in her life. Ethan always drove the cars with gears on their trips to Europe. He had tried to teach her once, but she had ignored every word, too distracted by the scenery.

Her fingers hovered over her phone. Should she call Ethan? Gina? Anyone?

She tried Gina first. No signal.

Damn.

Could she go back and exchange the car? Would they have an automatic one? Not sure.

She peeked out at the rental counter. The line was still massive. She was not willing to wait another hour again. The rain continued hammering against the windshield. It was getting dark. She couldn't sit here all night.

Gina's voice echoed in her head. "Don't die."

Maya smirked. "I'll try my best."

Taking a deep breath, she grabbed the gear stick.

Alright, Maya. You can do this.

She lurched forward. Then stopped. Lurched again. Stalled. Tried again.

Eventually, she figured out the rhythm when the engine howled, she shifted gears. By some miracle, she managed to navigate out of the lot.

The map she was given looked like something a child had drawn. One single loop around the island. A red X marked her accommodation. It looked simple, right? Except, the "highway" was a dirt road. No streetlights. No signs. Just thick jungle on either side, palm trees leaning over the path, and their shadows stretching in the dimming light. The rain made the road muddy, and it was full of potholes. She moved

20 miles per hour, like an 80-year-old; she always complained about being back home. Twice, monkeys darted across the road. Twice, Maya nearly screamed. She gripped the wheel, knuckles white. What if she got stuck here? What if her tire bursts? Her heart pounded. This was insane. By that time, it was pitch dark outside. The road seemed to never end. Why had she come here? This was too much to handle. By that time, she just wanted to crawl under her beloved blanket on her couch at home and feel the safety around her. It was overwhelming, and her nerves were shot.

Just as she started spiraling, a wooden sign appeared up ahead. She almost missed it and could barely read it in the dark. Red letters were carved into the planks.

WELCOME TO NATURA PARADISE.

Relief flooded her.

She had made it.

Barely.

She parked haphazardly, grabbed her suitcase, and stumbled into the main building.

It was empty, except for a single letter under a dim light.

Her name was on it.

Welcome, Maya. Lodge 7.

Beside it, a key.

She took it, stepping back into the rain in search of her accommodation. When she finally got there and stepped into the room, she was completely soaked, exhausted, overwhelmed by the colorful crowd at the airport, by the strange car, by the dark pothole jungle path, and by the arrival at her final destination. She felt she did not belong. But here she was. And whether she was ready or not, her journey had just begun.

ARRIVAL

12

CUT FROM THE OUTER WORLD

The rain was drumming, no, hammering on the wooden roof above her. Loud. Relentless. Like it was trying to wake the island itself. Maya stirred, half-asleep, suspended between dream and reality. For a brief moment, she didn't know where she was. The bed beneath her felt unfamiliar. The air, humid and heavy, clung to her skin like a second blanket.

She blinked into the dim light. She saw wood around her. Wooden walls, wooden table, a wooden wardrobe, wooden window frames, a wooden door, even her bed and side table were made out of wood.

The lodge was small, simple, raw, and bare. No plush duvets, no signature scent diffusers, no silent minibars, and no air conditioning, as she was used to from her business travels. The walls were decorated with a kind of handmade sculpture of blue butterflies. It was vivid and slightly crooked. The kind that could only be made by someone who wasn't trying to impress anyone. A fan buzzed overhead, creaking with each rotation, fighting a losing battle against the thick island heat. And yet, somehow, she had slept deeply.

She tried to piece it all together. Fragments of yesterday came slowly back, like waves lapping at her memory. The flight. The bumpy drive through a jungle road that barely qualified as a path. Her exhaustion had been absolute. She remembered stumbling upon a key with her name tied to it, the door creaking open, and then ... nothing. She couldn't even remember making it into bed. Her suitcase was still lying in the middle of the floor, unzipped and untouched like evidence.

Now, the silence of the island, broken only by the rain, felt both unnerving and sacred. She got up, disoriented. Her body felt stiff. Maybe there was coffee? Her head was still full of exhaustion, the kind that lives in your bones. But a quick search of the lodge revealed no machine either, no pods, no espresso shot to save her from this tropical inertia.

She found the bathroom, which was more of a cubicle. It had a toilet, a shower, and a tiny sink beneath an aging mirror. Her reflection startled her. Black smudges of yesterday's mascara haunted her eyes, and her hair was knotted into a wild crown of chaos.

"I look like a raccoon that lost its will to live," she muttered.

She instinctively grabbed her phone.

11:07 AM She had slept through the morning.

No signal.

Wait.

No. Signal.

She lifted the phone higher.

Stood on her toes like a desperate antenna.

Walked in a circle.

Nothing.

A sudden, sharp spike of panic clawed at her chest. Her heart raced. This couldn't be real. She rushed to the door and stepped out. The rain greeted her in thick, heavy sheets. The sky was a dense blanket of gray. Jungle-green trees bowed under the downpour. Somewhere in the distance, the sea must have been roaring too.

She stretched her arm into the rain, phone in hand, willing a bar of signal into existence.

Still nothing.

"What kind of place in the world has no signal?" she whispered, staring at the phone in her palm. "How does one even exist without the Internet?"

A ridiculous thought. Her body responded like she'd been denied oxygen. No emails. No messages. No feed to scroll through. No tiny dopamine hits from likes and reactions and endless information streams.

Just... her.

And the rain.

Her thumbs hovered over the screen, still out of habit. Her mind was already bargaining: Maybe the router is just out, maybe the rain storm knocked something out, maybe there's a reception desk with a hotspot.

But deep down, she knew.

This place was deliberately disconnected and intentionally off-grid.

And that terrified her.

It wasn't just about emails. It felt like her identity had just been stolen from her. She wasn't Maya-the-high-achiever, the executive, the inbox warrior without her digital lifeline.

Who was she here, without replies, reactions, or reminders of her importance?

She leaned against the lodge's damp doorway, watching the

rain blur the jungle. She couldn't remember the last time she had been without connection for more than a few hours.

No signal meant no validation.

No scrolling through the curated perfection of other people's lives.

No pretending.

This was a withdrawal.

From the outside world. From herself.

She didn't like the silence that filled the void.

Not yet.

But something deep inside, something buried beneath exhaustion, burnout, and boardroom wars, sighed.

A tiny, rebellious part of her whispered, *What if this is exactly what you needed?*

She thought of her best friend, Gina.

"Don't open the laptop. Don't look at your emails. Best turn off WI-Fi," she said.

Here we go, Gina. You got your will. I am disconnected.

No one could reach her.

And suddenly, that felt like a gift.

13

THE WOMAN WHO SAW

Maya groaned and dragged herself toward the shower, hoping the water might wake her up. As she turned the handle, a frigid cascade slammed against her back. She yelped and twisted the knob furiously. Nothing changed. It was still cold and, with time, turned lukewarm.

"Great. No hot water either," she muttered, teeth clenched with her body bracing.

There was one advantage: it jolted her awake. Maybe it was the slap she needed. She dried off and pulled on a summer dress, her favorite flip-flops, and looked around the lodge. No coffee in sight.

Her stomach rumbled in protest, and she realized she hadn't eaten in... who knows how long. Maybe she could still catch breakfast. Or at least a piece of bread and, hopefully, find a miracle WI-Fi hotspot hidden in some forgotten corner.

She opened the door. The rain hadn't stopped. If anything, it had intensified. It was a tropical downpour converting the island into a wet blur. Maya grabbed the plastic bag she had packed around her shoes and threw it over her head in the hope she would not get as wet as yesterday again. She sprinted toward the main house, slipping along the muddy path, with the plastic bag flapping like a ridiculous rain hat. The door was slightly ajar and creaking softly in the wind. She stepped inside, dripping and breathless.

The room was still and empty. A long wooden table stretched across the center beautifully in a raw, unfinished kind of way, with one plate and cutlery on it. Other than that, there were no signs, no buffet trays, and no chirpy staff with name tags.

Suddenly, Maya heard some noise. A female loud voice singing in a language Maya didn't understand, echoing from somewhere beyond the walls.

"Hello?" she called.

Nothing.

The voice continued, full-throated and unapologetic. Who-ever it was, she was completely immersed in her song. The clatter of pots and pans joined in like percussion.

"Hello?" Maya tried again, louder.

Still no reaction.

She hesitated. Her stomach made a dramatic growl in protest, and she took a breath.

"HELLO, MISS?!"

The singing stopped mid-note. Maya heard footsteps approaching her. An older woman appeared in the doorway like a wave of warmth from an unexpected fireplace. Round, radiant, colorful glasses slipping down her nose and an apron tied haphazardly. She wore a grin so wide it looked like it had been etched into her face years ago and simply never left.

"Welcome, Maya!" she sang in broken English. "You here! Good! Very good!"

Before Maya could respond, the woman wrapped her in an enormous, tight, warm, and overwhelming hug. Maya stiffened. She didn't do hugs. Especially not with strangers. And definitely not before coffee.

And why did this woman know her name?

When the woman finally pulled away, her eyes sparkled like she'd just found a long-lost daughter.

"I, Maria. Your friend!" she declared, as if it were the most natural thing in the world.

Your... what?

Maya blinked. A polite, stunned smile stretched across her lips.

"Uh. Hi."

"You okay?" Maria asked. Her eyes were steady and full of something Maya couldn't quite name. It was not pity and not concern. It was her full presence. The kind that sees through you. It made her feel uncomfortable.

Maya blinked and looked away, caught off guard. She wasn't used to being looked at like that. She was seen, not assessed. It made her feel strangely exposed, like someone had cracked the armor she didn't even know she was wearing.

"I... yeah, I'm okay," Maya muttered, though she wasn't entirely sure she meant it.

Maria beamed even brighter. *How was that even possible?*

"Breakfast?" Maya asked, cautiously hopeful.

She even mimed the universal eating gesture, lifting her hand towards her mouth, just in case Maria would not understand.

Maria's face lit up with understanding.

"Ah! Yes. Come!"

She gestured for Maya to sit at the big table where the plate and cutlery were set and disappeared into the kitchen again.

Her footsteps were accompanied by the renewed clatter of pots and a few off-key notes of her earlier song.

Maya sat down, dazed. Maria had set the table for her as if she'd been waiting for her all morning.

Moments later, Maria returned with a feast. She carried a tray overflowing with astonishing tropical fruits, Maya had never seen, thick toast with what appeared to be homemade jam, a glass of fresh orange juice, and, blessedly, hot, aromatic coffee. There was even a handwritten note tucked beside the plate: *Maya.*

Maria put the tray on the table in front of Maria and plopped into the chair across from her, watching with obvious satisfaction as Maya bit into a juicy slice of mango.

Maria didn't move. She didn't fuss around the kitchen. She just sat there. Watching. Smiling. It felt like when Maya was a child and her mother was watching her eat. It was unsettling. Since Ethan left, breakfast had been whatever she could grab between emails. Sometimes just coffee. Sometimes nothing at all. No one made her breakfast. Nor sat across from her. No one waited to see if she ate. No one noticed.

This woman, this stranger, was staring at her like she was the most important person in the world.

Doesn't she have other things to do? Other guests?

Apparently not.

"Good?" Maria asked.

Maya nodded slowly, sipping her second cup of coffee. "Good."

Then, because the digital itch in her soul wouldn't be silenced any longer, she took a breath and asked the question that had been gnawing at her.

"Do you have WI-Fi?"

69

Maria blinked. Then smiled. Then laughed, a belly-deep, full-body laugh.

"No. No."

Maya tried again. "But maybe... later? When the rain stops?"

Maria's face broke into an even wider grin.

"No. No," she said again, cheerfully, as if she were announcing the lunch menu.

Maya just stared at her.

How is this funny? This is not funny. This is a disaster!

No connection. No posts. No updates. No news. No emails.

The outer world had disappeared.

Maria simply smiled, as Maya's question had been answered.

With a light touch on Maya's shoulder, gentle, almost maternal, Maria turned and made her way back to the kitchen, singing again mixed with the clatter of dishes and the rhythm of the rain. Maya sat alone at the long wooden table, the empty coffee cup warm in her hands, the fruit plate picked clean. Her stomach was full, but something else inside her still gnawed.

The rain drummed steadily outside. No WI-Fi. No phone signal. No plan.

She looked around the quiet room, unsure of what to do next.

For the first time in a long time, nothing was demanding her attention.

And that, strangely, was the most uncomfortable part of all.

Why am I so terrified to do nothing?

Who am I if I am not working?

Who am I without my job?

She had no answers.

Not yet.

14

THE PATH OF LEAST EXPECTATION

The rain had softened into a steady whisper, like the island was sighing in its sleep. Maya got up from the big, long breakfast table, stood under the awning of the main house, arms crossed, staring out into the gray blur beyond. Her stomach was full, her coffee had kicked in, and yet she felt twitchy and restless. Her body hadn't gotten the memo yet that this place didn't run on back-to-back meetings and never-ending notifications.

No phone. No signal. No WI-Fi. Just rain. And time. And nothing scheduled.

She had no idea what to do with that kind of freedom.

I need to do something. I cannot just sit here. Maybe I walk, she thought, more out of rebellion than curiosity.

There wasn't a clear path ahead. It was just a squishy trail of wet earth that seemed to loop behind the lodges and toward the jungle. A "no-go zone" in her old life. Too unknown. Too risky. Too unfamiliar. But here? It was either that or sit at the table and stare out of the window like a lost houseplant.

So she stepped into the drizzle. Her flip-flops slapping

against her heels, and her dress clinging slightly to her legs. The air smelled like rain and wet leaves and something vaguely citrusy.

The path was narrow and uneven, winding through a cluster of overgrown bushes and a tangled curtain of vines. Trees arched above her like giant question marks. Their dripping leaves were tickling her shoulders as she passed. A low croak echoed from somewhere deep in the green.

She told herself she wasn't nervous.

But she was.

Was it the unfamiliar jungle?

Was it the unclear end of the path?

Was it her stillness?

Of not knowing what this walk was for.

Of not having an agenda.

Of not having a goal.

She wasn't used to moving without a mission.

She wasn't sure this was a good idea anymore.

And then ...Her foot slid. One second, she was upright. Next, she knew she was on the ground. She landed on her side in a patch of warm, sticky mud. Her left flip-flop gave up the will to live and snapped in half like a defeated soldier. The mud had claimed her flip-flop as its sacrifice.

Maya lay there for a moment, staring up at the pale sky through the dripping leaves. The rain was tapping gently on her cheeks. And then, she laughed loudly. It was the kind of laugh that bubbles up from somewhere unexpected. Not because it was funny. But it was so absurd. She was a woman who had once presented quarterly revenue forecasts to global boardrooms in designer heels. And now?

She was barefoot, muddy, and alone on a forgotten island

with no WI-Fi and a broken shoe.

It was ridiculous.

It was amazing.

It was ridiculously amazing.

She sat up, wiped the mud from her arm with the edge of her dress, and pulled off the other flip-flop. Useless. She put them both into her plastic bag, which used to be her umbrella.

This was enough adventure for her today. Then, barefoot, she turned around and walked back. The ground was warm and soft beneath her feet. Every step squished. She slowed down. And for the first time since arriving, she noticed with full presence her surroundings. She spotted a single red crab darting sideways into a hole. A leaf the size of her head fluttered gently down in front of her, twirling like a dancer. A line of ants carrying a tiny yellow flower petal. A tangle of vines twisted into a perfect spiral. And there, right in front of her, a big blue butterfly, she had never seen before. The delicate blue wings were resting on the edge of a stone. None of it was asking for attention. None of it was curated for likes. It was just there. Maya crouched, barefoot and filthy, and stared at the butterfly. It didn't move. Neither did she.

And for an instant in time, there was no deadline, no inbox, no strategy to save the company, and no reputation to protect. Just a woman in the jungle, and a blue butterfly that didn't need her to be anything. Just Maya's full presence in the here and now. It was a beautiful moment. It was magical.

Eventually, the rain picked up again. She stood up, her dress was covered in mud, and her hair was a wild halo of tangled curls. She didn't know where she was exactly, but somehow, she wasn't afraid anymore and trusted she would find her way back to the lodges. She kept walking, barefoot and smiling to herself, giddy, like someone who knew a secret.

She had stepped into the jungle looking for something to do and walked out with something far more precious: the quiet knowing that being was already enough.

15

COCOON

By the time Maya stumbled back into her lodge, she looked like a woman who had walked through a storm, and in a way, she had. Wet hair clung to her cheeks, her dress was caked in mud, so was her skin, and her broken flip-flop dangled from her fingers like a soggy reminder that nothing about this trip was going according to plan. And strangely, that thought didn't bother her as much as it would have back home.

She stripped off the soggy clothes, took a quick shower, and wrapped herself in a towel. Her suitcase still lay half-unpacked on the floor. She rummaged through it and pulled out an oversized T-shirt, which was soft from years of use. Her fingers were wrinkled from the rain, and her bare feet left little prints on the wooden floor.

The room was quiet. Almost too quiet for Maya. She was used to the constant sound of honking cars and distant sirens in the city. She reached into her bag and pulled out her emergency snacks, a bruised banana, a half-eaten granola bar, and a handful of almonds. Not exactly dinner, but somehow, it felt enough. She curled onto the bed, legs tucked beneath her, and nibbled slowly on her food, looking out the window into the mist-covered jungle.

Maya stared at the wooden ceiling, feeling the weight of the stillness settle over her like a second blanket. And another feeling crawled right beside. Guilt. Guilt of leaving her colleagues hanging.

Everyone back home is probably on their 10th Zoom call by now, she thought.

The inbox must be overflowing with tons of messages labeled "urgent" that never really were. Poor Andrea, probably scrambling to clean up her mess. Richard, probably fuming and barking orders. Someone is probably talking over her in a meeting. Someone else is asking for her strategy. She imagined the glass-walled boardroom. The buzz of tension. The relentless grind.

Maya, where are you?

She wasn't sure she knew the answer anymore. What she did know was: She was stuck on an island. Alone. Eating almonds in an oversized T-shirt.

What the hell am I doing here? I don't belong here.

She closed her eyes.

And then, the jungle came back to her. Her eyes fluttered closed, and behind them, the image of this magical moment on that muddy path returned. The trees surrounding her were enormous. She remembered this wonderful, majestic blue butterfly. She has never seen such a big and beautiful creature. It had landed so quietly on that stone. Wings like stained glass. Fragile. Weightless. Completely still.

But she knew what it had gone through to get there.

People always talked about butterflies as symbols of freedom. Of grace. Of transformation.

They made it sound so beautiful.

A flutter of wings. A lightness in the air. The final stage, glorious and delicate.

But no one ever talked about what came before.

No one talked about the cocoon. The absolute undoing.

Maya's eyes stayed closed as the thought unfolded inside her, slow and heavy.

Before being this glorious and delicate butterfly, it was a cater-pillar.

The caterpillar doesn't just grow wings.

It doesn't stretch and emerge stronger in stages.

No, it breaks itself down. It melts into a biological soup inside its own body.

All its structure is gone.

Every single cell is turning to liquid chaos.

Nothing is left of what it was. No legs. No form. No control.

Just goo.

Can you imagine?

To let go so completely of who you were—

To surrender everything without knowing what you'll become.

That was the part people skip over. The part we don't post on Instagram.

The mess. The confusion. The not-knowing.

And yet, it was necessary.

You can't become a butterfly by staying a caterpillar.

There's no shortcut. No cheat code. No clean version.

You have to go through the dark.

You have to disappear.

You have to trust the breakdown.

Maya's chest rose and fell beneath the blanket, her breath

quiet now, but steady.

Is that what's happening to me? she wondered.

She wasn't who she was back home, not anyone's inspirational award winner, not the powerhouse executive, not anyone's boss. She felt empty, tired, and exhausted. Right now, she was simply a woman without any makeup, cuddled in her bed. She was goo. Undone. And maybe that was okay.

The jungle was still out there. Alive. Breathing. And so was she. Wrapped in silence, she let her eyes close. Thoughts slowing. Muscles melting into the mattress. She was exhausted and surrendered.

Tomorrow will come.

But tonight?

She was in her own cocoon.

And maybe, just maybe, falling apart is okay.

And maybe, it is the first step to something more beautiful and majestic.

16

THE DAY THE WAVES TOOK IT ALL

When Maya awoke the next morning, the birds were having a full-on jungle gossip session outside. You could hear the chirps, clicks, and fluttering wings. It was a wild orchestra playing the soundtrack from somewhere far. Far from the noise she was used to. City traffic. Desperate honking. Screaming sirens.

She blinked into the golden light of the sun that danced across her face. It had pushed its way through layers of thick jungle canopy, wriggled through the gaps in the wooden lodge, and landed softly on her cheeks like a gentle nudge.

Her body refused to move. It clung to the bed like a lifeline. Her limbs were heavy. Every inch of her said, *not yet.*

Still on autopilot, her hand reached for her phone, a reflex hardwired into her brain. But when the screen lit up, all she saw was nothing. No messages. No alerts. No connection. Just silence, echoing back at her from the middle of nowhere.

She stared at the clock. It was noon.

"No way..." she murmured aloud. She had slept for sixteen hours straight. The last time she'd slept even eight hours was...

what, college? Her usual nights were five-hour marathons of tossing, turning, and waking up to the sound of her alarm clock, a signal for starting the corporate war. She'd been living in fear, fear of missing out, of not achieving, of disappointing. That fear had fueled her for years.

But today, there was no alarm.

She was disconnected.

Cut off.

She felt empty.

Drained.

Done. Rock-bottom tired not just her body, but her soul.

The sunlight grew stronger, creeping deeper into the lodge. It warmed the wooden floor, now glowing honey-gold instead of rain-beaten brown. Everything looked different. Softer. More alive. The hammock on the porch swayed gently, like it was breathing.

Her stomach grumbled. She reached into her bag and crunched the last of her chips. Not exactly the breakfast she dreamed of on a tropical escape, but enough to get her moving.

The cold shower hit her sharply again. Yesterday, she cursed it. Today, she didn't mind.

She slipped into her favorite soft cotton ocean blue summer dress and slid into her shoes. No plans. No agenda. No "To-Do" list. Just another day.

As she walked out of her lodge, she saw a blue butterfly on a leaf again. Like a sign. It shimmered in its electric blue, which felt unreal.

Good morning, sunshine, it seemed to whisper.

There's a whole new world out there, waiting just for you.

The jungle beyond the butterfly was lush, wild, alive, as if it were waiting for her. She walked over to the main hall. The reception was quiet. Today, there was no singing of Maria. No clatter of cups. No trace of her mysterious host. So Maya decided to follow the path again, the same one from yesterday, but this time with new eyes.

Rain had carved puddles into the ground, sparkling like mirrors. Mosquitoes danced above them.

"Should've put mosquito spray on," she muttered.

She kept walking. Ants marched across her path, like a miniature parade. She paused to watch it and marveled at their silent teamwork and their incredible unspoken coordination.

Then she almost walked face-first into a spider web.

"Whoa!" she yelped, stumbling back as a fat spider glared at her from the corner.

"Nope. I am definitely not your dinner today," she said.

She kept walking, passing the place where she slipped and decided to turn around yesterday. This time, she wanted to go beyond that point and discover more.

After a while of walking, she heard a new sound. A deep, powerful rhythm. Not threatening. Not wild. But welcoming. She pushed through the final tree branches, and there it was.

The ocean.

It opened up like a secret revealed. A wide, wild, untouched stretch of white sand, kissed by waves of the turquoise water and crowned with a cloudless blue sky. No tourists were in sight, no sun umbrellas, no screaming children, no teenage music, or lovers making memories. Just a lonely surfer riding the waves out in the ocean, fitting right into the idyllic scenery.

The beach shimmered under the sun, the sea breathing in and out in slow, rhythmic sighs. She stood still, heart full and empty at once. To the right, she saw a shipwreck, half-buried in the sand. Time had devoured it. Faded wood. Peeling paint. Rusted edges. The red and blue hulls peeked through like forgotten dreams. She walked toward it slowly.

This ship didn't have only one leak. It had cracks everywhere. It was weathered. Its body was hollowed out by too many battles. It must have once sailed proudly, fiercely and with purpose. But storms had stripped it bare. Its mast pointed nowhere now. And here it rested in peace, quiet and forgotten.

Like her.

A wreck washed ashore by storms, she tried so hard to navigate.

Rusting from the years she spent holding it all together.

Splintered by expectations she undeniably agreed to.

This wasn't just a ship.

It was her reflection.

Tears came suddenly, hot and unapologetic. All the emotions she kept inside for so many years seemed to flow without limit. She didn't wipe them away. They carved paths down her cheeks as she turned to the sea and to the endless horizon, where the sky and water met in a quiet promise.

Somewhere out there was her life.

Richard barking orders like salt in a wound.

Andrea dutifully reminded her of what she owed.

Her mother's doubt rang louder and louder.

And Ethan, who had already given up on her.

She had carried all of it.

For too long.

The pressure.

The noise.

The invisible checklist of who she had to be: perfect, poised, and productive.

And now the waves came for it.

Each crash against the rocks was a sacred rhythm.

A whisper with weight.

We'll take it from here.

You don't need to hold this anymore.

The ocean didn't ask. It just pulled.

With every tide, it reached into her chest and gently tugged.

Tugged at the shame behind the deadlines.

Tugged at the guilt for never being enough.

Tugged at the exhaustion that had hardened her spirit.

Each wave unraveled the tight knot inside her, one thread at a time.

The sea can have it all.

Richard's disapproval.

Andrea's quiet plea.

Her mother's sharp tone.

Ethan's dismissal.

All of it dissolved, memory by memory, into saltwater, carried far into the blue sky

until they were no more than specks swallowed by sunlight.

The knot loosened.

And something shifted.

A lightness entered.

A hollow space where heaviness once lived.

The ocean had seen a thousand souls like hers.

Tired captains of ships that had lost their course.

She was just one of them.

The sun reached through the sky, wrapped her in golden arms,

and whispered, *Welcome back.*

Her skin hummed. Her breath deepened. Her heart opened, like petals once closed in fear.

She tilted her face to the sky, soaking it in.

Like a phone once dead, it finally gets connected to a charger.

Her battery started to flicker again and glowed.

She looked at the shipwreck one last time.

But this time, she didn't see herself.

That ship had ended its journey here.

She hadn't.

Maybe she had lost her map.

Maybe she'd dropped anchor in the wrong harbor.

Maybe she drifted too far, for too long.

But her journey was not over yet.

She wiped her tears. Smiled softly.

"Thank you for listening to me!

Thank you for taking my sorrows away at this moment.

Thank you for letting me breathe again," she said quietly to the ocean.

And suddenly, Maya heard the whisper again.

There's a whole new world out there, waiting just for you!

17

THE GIFT OF A COCONUT

The sand was warm beneath Maya's feet and soft like powdered sugar. The ocean hummed beside her. She walked slowly, without purpose, a map, or a plan. She just followed wherever the shore would take her.

And then, around a rocky bend, she saw her. An old woman bent with age, barefoot, skin sun-kissed and wrinkled like waves carved into time. She must have been in her 70s, but dressed in a colorful dress with flowers stamped on it. Her hair was pulled into a loose bun, streaked with silver and salt. She sat under the shade of a palm tree, beside a wooden cart barely held together by twine and nails. The cart was filled with coconuts. Some were green. Some were brown. One was already halfway open under her machete.

How could that old lady still be working under that heat? She must have worked for decades already. Maya thought.

The woman seemed not to mind. It seemed she was enjoying it. She was humming. A tune Maya didn't recognize, but it wrapped around her like a lullaby. She cut into the coconut with steady, practiced hands. Each movement was graceful and deliberate, like a ritual passed down through generations.

Maya couldn't find a sign advertising her product and prices. No sales announcement was heard. Just an old woman. A simple cart. And the ocean breeze.

Maya stood there for a moment, watching her. The woman looked up, and her face split into a warm smile seeing her. Some teeth were missing. She raised a hand in greeting, as if they already knew each other. Maya looked around to see if there was somebody else besides her. There was none. She must have meant her. Maya stepped closer.

"Hi," she said, unsure if the woman spoke English.

The woman nodded. "Coco?"

Maya realized she didn't have anything to eat except her crackers, nor anything to drink. She suddenly craved some liquid and solid food. She answered.

"Yes, please."

The machete sliced through the shell with a confident thwack. The top popped open. The woman handed Maya the coconut with both hands. She had rough palms but a gentle touch. There was no straw with it. Just a small, hand-carved wooden scoop. Natural and pure.

Maya took a sip. The coconut water was cold, slightly sweet, and tasted like nothing she'd ever had in the city.

She responded with a smile: "Thank you!"

Maya sat down on the sand beside the cart without asking. The woman didn't mind. They sat in silence for a few minutes.

The woman pointed toward the sea. "Every day," she said in a soft, accented voice. The sun comes. The sun goes. I stay. Happy."

Maya tilted her head. "You do this every day?"

The woman nodded. "Long time. My mother. Her mother, too."

She pointed to her cart with a soft laugh. "Not big. But enough."

Maya looked at the cart. It was old, weathered, and patched up in places. Nothing fancy. Nothing branded. Maya nodded slowly, but her mind had already begun spinning. She could see it. A brand. A business. A story to pitch. "Island Wisdom" fresh coconut water from paradise. Eco-friendly packaging. A logo inspired by the old woman's hands. Distributing it through wellness cafes, yoga studios, and boutique hotel minibars. A purpose-driven company that helps someone like her. Maya imagined setting the woman up with a proper stand. Solar-powered. Hygienic. Then a production chain. Export deals. Maybe even a feature in a business magazine about "Empowering Indigenous Local Entrepreneurs." For a flicker of a second, she was back in her power suit, presenting a deck to investors, convincing them that coconuts could change lives.

She looked back at the woman.

"Don't you want more?" Maya asked gently. "A bigger stand? More customers?"

The woman chuckled. Her eyes were sparkling. She tapped her heart.

"I have what I need."

Still humming. Still smiling. Still present.

She was not dreaming of shipping containers far away, or having a fancy website, or the next expansion. She was just happy with what she had. It was enough for her. Maya blinked. The woman gestured toward the beach, the sea, and the sun.

"People come. People go. Want too much. Rush too fast. Don't see what is here."

Maya swallowed hard. She realized, with a thud in her chest, that this impulse to build, to scale, and to optimize was the very thing she had come here to escape.

The woman didn't need saving.

She already had something Maya didn't: joy.

Maya had spent years chasing more. More meetings. More promotions. More followers. More applause. More titles. More team members. She believed happiness was waiting for her at the end. But here was this woman, with a cart of coconuts and a machete, who seemed to have found joy where Maya hadn't even thought to look.

So instead of pitching a plan, Maya just stood, placed her hand over her heart, and bowed her head slightly.

"Thank you," she said again.

The woman smiled.

"Coco good?" she asked, chuckling.

Maya grinned. "The best."

Maya sat there for a long time drinking her coconut slowly and eating the coconut meat, letting the salt breeze kiss her face. She watched the woman serve one local boy, and then a couple passing by. She had no rush and no pressure. She just seemed happy to serve others her coconuts. She did not seem to mind her past working hard for decades, nor did she mind the future building an empire. She seemed to be content with her presence.

When it was time to go, Maya stood and placed a few coins in the woman's hand. The woman shook her head.

"Gift," she said. "My gift to you."

Maya's throat tightened. "Thank you."

The woman pointed to her heart.

"Be happy," she said simply. "Be here. Not there." Maya

nodded. And for the first time, she didn't think of what had happened before she arrived here, nor what was awaiting her when she would go home.

She was here and felt happy. She walked away with no pitch deck and no business plan for another Coconut Enterprise. Instead, she walked away with something far more precious in her heart: Inner peace right where she was.

18

A THOUSAND SENSATIONS

Maya woke up the next day. It was already her fourth day on the island. Yesterday had unraveled more than she expected. That walk through the jungle, the ocean, the shipwreck, and the beach walk. It had drained her emotionally. Like something heavy had finally been washed away.

She still couldn't get the old woman selling coconuts out of her head. That peaceful grin. The cart of coconuts. The way she had laughed, not because life was perfect, but because she had found a way to be happy with her life as it was.

And then there was Maria waiting for her last night, as if she'd known Maya would come back from the beach empty and starving. There had been a sandwich on a plate. Just what she needed. Maya had collapsed onto the bed afterwards, still dressed, and passed out into what could only be described as a coma, burnt by the sun and emotion.

This morning, she felt different. Lighter. And hungry again. She decided it was time to get some groceries and stop living off Maria's kindness. She threw on a dress, tied her damp hair into a messy bun, and wandered to the main house.

The breakfast room was buzzing today. Maya blinked. She hadn't seen this many people in this place since her arrival. She realized, for the first time, she had made it in time for breakfast. Maria spotted her instantly. Her smile was wide and warm.

"Here you are, sunshine! Come, join us!" she beamed, gesturing toward the long communal table already brimming with food and conversation. Maya hesitated. All the seats were full. All except one. Maria didn't give her a choice. She took a plate, a napkin, and cutlery. A full mug of coffee appeared like magic. Maria had cleared the way.

Maya sat down with all the other guests. She was not used to sitting at a table with strangers. Eight fellow travelers were gathered around the table: a family juggling two chaotic toddlers, a couple glowing with just-married energy, and two middle-aged men arguing passionately over island hiking trails. It was loud and human and somehow, it felt okay.

She reached for a piece of fresh bread, added some jam, and grabbed a mango slice.

The man who was just planning the next hike with his partner next to her turned around.

"Good morning!" He said with a booming voice and a crinkled smile.

"I'm Gregg. Nice to meet you!"

Maya blinked. "Hi. I'm Maya."

The rest of the table chimed in, cheerful and unbothered by formality. No one asked what she did. No one cared about her hair or makeup. No one mentioned titles. No LinkedIn-worthy intros. No pitches for the next hot idea. It was oddly refreshing.

There she was, in the middle of nowhere, chatting with strangers from who-knows-where, all sitting at the same table, passing bread and jam like old friends. She couldn't imagine this ever happening back home. Back there, even neighbors in the elevator avoided eye contact, silently sipping their take-out coffee cups in the hopes of not being bothered by anybody. Back home, she is rushing through the day without wanting to talk to her colleagues. She had to think of Andrew, the accountant, back in her office, whom she had ignored the other day.

After a few bites and a refill of coffee, she remembered her mission. She turned to Gregg.

"Hey, is there a supermarket nearby? I'm hoping to get a few groceries."

Gregg smiled with a hint of mischief.

"Ah, yes. Just follow the gravel road for about a kilometer. Turn right. There's a little village. The market is right in the center. You'll find it."

"Great. Thanks," she said, rising from the table with her backpack slung over one shoulder.

"Enjoy!" Gregg added, with that same smile that now clearly translated to: *You're in for something.*

She followed the road exactly as instructed. It was hot and dusty. The sun was brutal. Only the shadow of the palm trees gave her relief. After about twenty minutes, the path opened up to a small village.

And there it was: the so-called market. But this wasn't like a supermarket she knew from home. There were no sleek aisles. No branded packaging. No barcode scanners. No towering shelves stacked with duplicates of everything. No signs labeled "Gluten-Free" or "Low-Fat." No background music playing at just the right volume. No air conditioning humming in the background. No signs where to find the baking products or soft drinks. This wasn't anything Maya had ever seen. The moment she stepped under a colorful bamboo archway, the world exploded. Noise. Color. Smell. Chaos. Life. She froze for a beat. This wasn't a normal grocery shopping chore. This was an ambush of the senses.

A thousand things happened at once. The *smell* hit first. It was a chaotic orchestra of fruit, spice, fire, fish, and something that could only be described as "mystery meat." Smoke drifted lazily from open fires. Mangoes, pineapples, and bananas were stacked like pyramids beside skewers of meat, trays of bright chilies, and, wait, were those crickets? Yes. Crickets. Something with legs that definitely used to fly. Her stomach wasn't sure if it should growl or retreat.

Then the sound hit her. Bartering voices, clanging pots, bursts of laughter, a radio playing a song she didn't know but kind of loved. Children dashed between stalls, barefoot and fearless, giggling like they owned the place. People were everywhere, alive, noisy, and radiant. Vendors waved her over with wild enthusiasm, holding up fruits and sticks with fried things. A woman in a bright floral shirt took Maya's hand and gave her a wobbly orange cube on a stick.

"Taste! You try! Very good!"

And before Maya could politely decline, it was in her hand.

She tried it. It was sweet. Chewy. Slightly spicy.

"What was that?" she mumbled, mouth still half-full.

The woman just laughed.

Maya turned and nearly collided with a chicken. An actual chicken. Alive. Clucking. In a cage. For a moment, she remembered news of a bird flu somewhere on TV. She got frightened for a second but got distracted by a man sharpening a knife and puffing on a cigarette like it was just another Tuesday. She stumbled backwards and knocked into a towering basket of bananas.

"Sorry! Sorry!" she mumbled. The man chuckled and handed her one. No words. Just a banana. For free. She blinked.

Her brain could barely catch up. This wasn't a market. It was a celebration of everything at once. She realized how far away she was from home. She had travelled further than her parents ever did. If only they would know how different things are here.

She wandered, dazed, through the maze of stalls. A woman braided a strand of hibiscus into Maya's hair without asking. Another beckoned her toward glowing glass jars of what looked like jellyfish. An old man pounded herbs in a stone bowl the size of a beach ball.

She must've looked like an alien among them, pale, mani-cured, too clean, and too wide-eyed. She wore her best "tropical explorer" dress, matched with flip-flops and a sunhat that screamed "tourist". No one else looked like her. Everyone was sun-warmed, calloused, weathered like they belonged to the island.

And yet, no one made her feel out of place. They smiled. Nodded. Offered tastes. Giggled at her expressions. She felt no judgment. No questions asked about her job, her title, or her purpose for being here. They did not care. It wasn't about that.

She bought spices she didn't know how to use. Let a vendor henna a blue butterfly onto her wrist. Tried a fried scorpion and regretted it immediately. She laughed so hard, tears were running down her cheeks.

At one point, she sat down on a plastic stool beside a man grilling skewers over an open fire. He handed her a bowl. She didn't ask what it was. She just ate.

And something settled inside her. This place, this noisy, messy, unpredictable whirlwind, was alive. And so was she.

95

She thought of the grocery aisles back home. Everything plastic-wrapped, labeled, sanitized. Perfectly arranged and utterly lifeless.

And this? This was the opposite. Here, everything was too loud, too much, too bright, and exactly what she didn't know she needed.

She looked up at the crisscrossed tarps fluttering above and let the smells, the sounds, the people wash over her.

Paradise wasn't curated. It wasn't calm.

It was raw and real.

And today, it smelled like turmeric, sweat, grilled chicken, and mango.

And she wouldn't want it any other way.

19

THE COOKING LESSON SHE NEVER ASKED FOR

Maya returned from the market victorious and slightly sticky. Her backpack bulged with fruits she couldn't name, herbs she couldn't identify, and one suspicious-looking root that the vendor had sworn was "very good for energy," though, judging by his toothless grin and manic eyes, she wasn't entirely convinced.

She made her way back along the gravel path, sun on her back, sweat on her brow, and an unexpected lightness in her chest. She felt alive.

When she arrived back at the guesthouse, Maria was wiping down the big wooden table, humming a tune that sounded like it had no beginning and no end.

"Look at you!" she beamed as Maya stepped inside. Her damp hair was plastered to her forehead. Her heavy backpack slipped off one shoulder.

"You wrestle with a monkey?" Maria asked in her broken English.

"Something like that." Maya laughed.

She emptied her loot dramatically onto the kitchen counter. It looked like a tropical explosion: green papayas, purple beans, yellow fruits with spikes, and her suspiciously looking root.

Maria raised an eyebrow. "Planning to open a jungle pharmacy?"

"I just wanted to make a salad," Maya shrugged.

Maria reached into the pile and pulled up the energy root.

"This is not a vegetable. It's soap."

Maya blinked. "Wait. What?"

Maria laughed so hard she had to lean against the fridge.

"You bought a bar of soap, darling. Smells great!"

Maya buried her face in her hands. "Of course I did!"

Maria gently set the soap aside and examined the rest.

"But the rest? Not bad. You've got half the island here."

She clapped her hands. "Alright then. Cooking lesson time."

"What? Now?" Maya asked, glancing down at her sweaty self. She was not a cook at all. She could barely make spaghetti and was always too tired to cook after work. And besides, why waste all that time cooking only for her?

"Now," Maria said firmly.

"This kitchen is not just for breakfast, and you've got a lesson to learn."

As she would have read Maya's mind.

What followed could only be described as a beautiful disaster. Maria was fast, fearless, and completely unbothered by recipes. She threw in a handful of this, a squeeze of that, and a pinch of spice. Maya, meanwhile, chopped everything into unequal, confused chunks and kept forgetting where the knife was. At one point, she sneezed so violently from a spoonful of Maria's mystery chili that she nearly knocked over the papaya bowl.

"You're doing great," Maria said. "Like a real local who's never cooked before."

"Comforting," Maya muttered, wiping her nose with a paper towel.

But as the smells filled the room with garlic, lime, a hint of smoke, and heat, Maya felt something shift.

She wasn't following a plan.

She wasn't trying to impress.

She was just here.

Chopping mangoes. Stirring rice. Frying onions. Laughing with a woman who didn't care what she did for a living, only whether she was stirring the pot clockwise like she'd been told.

They finally sat at the little table by the open window, their plates piled high with what Maya suspected was the most tropical freestyle stir-fry ever made. She took a bite. And froze.

"Oh my god," she said, wide-eyed. "It's out of this world!"

It turned out delicious.

Maria raised her glass of water. "To jungle soap and surprise stir-fry."

Maya clinked hers against it. "To do things badly and survive."

They laughed at each other. They ate. They talked. They shared stories of their lives, not the polished, LinkedIn kind, but the real ones. Maria spoke about growing up on the island, about her mother's secret chili recipe, about heartbreak, healing, and how she once accidentally served a lizard instead of chicken to a tourist.

Maya found herself opening up in return and talked about work, about Ethan, and the moment she realized her high heels hurt more than her feet. She didn't tell everything, but she opened up more than she'd had to anyone in years.

And Maria just nodded. She didn't give advice. She didn't show pity. She just listened and was here for Maya.

As the sun dipped low behind the trees, casting golden stripes across the table, Maya leaned back in her chair and sighed.

"I haven't done this in... I don't know how long."

"Cooking?"

"Cooking. Talking. Eating. Taking time. And enjoying all of it to the fullest."

Maria gave her that look. The one that meant she'd already known that.

Then she smiled.

"Welcome back, Maya."

20

INTO THE WILD

Maya was sipping her third cup of coffee at the big table in the main house the next morning. The family had risen early and gone to the beach. The honeymoon couple was still tucked in the corner, wrapped in their own little world. Maya watched the world go by from the heart of the jungle. She heard the familiar crunch of footsteps on the gravel approaching.

Gregg and his partner Leo appeared as if they had walked straight out of the greenery itself. Gregg had that mischievous, twinkle-eyed look that meant either danger or adventure, and Leo was right behind him with a backpack slung casually over one shoulder.

"Morning, beauty," Gregg grinned. "Feel like stretching those city legs today?"

Maya raised an eyebrow, half-smiling. She had not made plans for today.

"Where to?"

Leo pointed toward the jungle, the way explorers might point to treasure on a map. "We're heading into the wild through the jungle in search of a waterfall and whatever else wants to meet us along the way. Are you in?"

There was no hesitation this time. No "maybe later" or "I should rest." Just a pull. An approval for the adventure rising from somewhere deep in her chest.

"Hell yes!" she jumped out of her chair.

She was surprised by her sudden answer. That was not her older self. She normally had her calendar booked out for weeks, and every single step was planned beforehand without space for deviation.

"Give me five minutes to get ready!"

She walked to her little lodge, slipped into her hiking outfit, grabbed her survival backpack, and was ready for the day's adventure with Gregg and Leo.

The trail began almost invisibly, swallowed by vines and oversized leaves, as if the jungle was deciding whether or not to let them in. Each step was a surrender to the unknown mud squelching beneath their feet, branches creaking overhead, the air thick and humming with life.

They hadn't gone far when Maya stopped, captivated by a scene unfolding at her feet. There they were again. The ants, big ones, like she had seen before on her path to the beach. But this time she paused and took the time to watch them for a longer while. There were not only a few. She detected hundreds, maybe even thousands, marching in a perfect line. Some were carrying a fragment of green leaves, many times larger than their body. One was even dragging a tiny piece of orange fruit. It was like watching a living river flow across the jungle floor. Leo crouched beside her.

"Ants have been here for over 100 million years, long before us. They can carry 50 - 200 times their own weight. And a fun fact, they actually have two stomachs, one for themselves and one for others to feed everyone," he whispered. "No ego. No complaints. They just do it."

"They're building something," Maya murmured.

Gregg pointed toward the base of a nearby tree. "See that mound? That's their city with tunnels, chambers, and whole underground systems. It is all built one piece at a time. But each single ant helped build it all together."

Maya's eyes followed the path of a single ant, weaving carefully between obstacles, never stopping, and never doubting. Just doing its part and trusting the whole.

Imagine what we could build if we stopped fighting over who's in charge, she thought. *If we just do what we were meant to do, no more, no less, without our egos in between in the boardroom, no pushing and pulling over strategies. Just a clear goal, and everyone joining in.*

The ants are wiser than we are, she thought. *While we destroy the forest, they quietly repair it, nourish it, and protect it. While we obsess over titles and power, ants shift direction without conflict when one sees a better way, the others simply follow. And unlike us with our insatiable hunger, they carry two stomachs, always ensuring there's enough for everyone. Maybe we've evolved our minds, but ants have mastered something we still struggle with: living as one. They don't compete, they complete.*

She stood, slowly brushing her hands on her shorts. The forest stretched ahead, dense, humming, and alive.

"I guess we keep walking," she said.

The jungle wrapped around them like a cathedral with high ceilings made of interlocking leaves, beams of golden light slanting through in places, illuminating pockets of wonder. It was wild and untouched. Branches tangled like curly hair, and roots burst through the earth like veins. Trees didn't follow the rules here. They bent, twisted, and reached in every direction to find light. Some leaned sideways. Some grew in spirals. Some broke through rock like nothing could stop them. No one trimmed them. No one ordered them into symmetry. And yet they grow, reaching for the sky. They belong.

There was no map and no master plan. No one here who tried to optimize their potential. They just grew naturally. They were beautiful in their imperfection. Maya ran her hand along the bark of one. They felt rough, solid, and ancient.

"These trees," she said softly. "They must have been here for centuries. They probably have seen everything, haven't they?"

Gregg nodded. "Storms. Droughts. Fires. Time."

Leo added, "And still, they stand. Not alone, though. Their roots are all connected. It is a hidden network beneath our feet. They feed each other, warn each other, and help each other grow."

Maya stood still, eyes wide. "One big living system."

"Exactly," Leo said. "One tree doesn't compete with the others. They all have their space. They rise together and belong together."

The words settled inside her like seeds.

What if that was strength? she thought. *Not standing out but standing together. Not growing fast, but growing deep.*

She tilted her head back and looked up at the canopy. The trees didn't rush. They didn't force it. They just grew toward light, around obstacles, grounded with their deep roots.

Maybe that's what I need, too.

To trust who she was.

To grow, knowing there's a supporting network around her.

To feel she belonged to a bigger community.

To stop walking the path someone else paved, and start carving her own.

A rustle overhead made them freeze.

"Look there!" Gregg said. "Do you see it?"

Leo and Maya squinted. "Where?"

Gregg pointed toward a branch. "There!"

"Ahh! Yes, I see it!" Leo said.

At first, Maya saw nothing. Just swaying leaves in the distance with sunlight flickering through. Then she saw a black spot. It was almost invisible. A sloth. Maya squealed softly, full of joy. She had never seen one before. It clung upside-down to a thick branch, not moving, except for the faintest turn of its head. It was not bothered by anything around. After a few peaceful moments of staring, the sloth stretched out one languid arm toward a nearby leaf. It didn't rush. I didn't worry. It didn't waste energy. It simply moved with precision, grace, and intention in order to get one leaf for one bite. That was enough. Maya watched in reverence.

"It only uses energy when it needs to," she whispered.

Gregg nodded. "Imagine how much we could save time, energy, and sanity if we only spent it where it mattered."

The sloth blinked, as if agreeing with Gregg's comment. And then went again. It wasn't lazy. It was wise.

And Maya, who had once prided herself on her high-speed, no-brake lifestyle, stood in the jungle, learning from a creature that had mastered the art of stillness.

Hours passed. Or maybe time simply stopped. The jungle grew thicker and wilder. They continued to walk. One step after another. Something inside Maya was calming her. She did not slow down in defeat but surrendered to the rhythm of the jungle.

Then she heard it. Faint at first. A rumble, like distant applause. The roar of water grew louder. They pushed through the final curtain of trees and stepped into a hidden oasis.

There it was. The waterfall they had been seeking. It was cascading from high rocks, crashing into a clear, turquoise pool. The mist was rising like incense. Maya gasped. The sound wasn't noise. It was power, movement, and life, finding its way. The river didn't ask for permission. It didn't wait for perfect conditions. It carved through stone, danced through roots, crashed, tumbled, and surged forward anyway. Sometimes gently. Sometimes with force. But always forward.

They dropped their bags, lay by the riverbank, and stared at the beauty before them. No one spoke. No one needed to. The jungle had spoken for them. Maya breathed in the fresh air. The warmth made her comfortable. She felt peaceful at this place. She walked to the edge of the water and dipped her toes into the cool water. She closed her eyes.

I am the river, she thought. *And I will also find my way.*

They ate their picnic lunch at the waterfall, jumped into the fresh water, and let their bodies dry in the sun, listening to the sounds of the jungle.

When the sun was getting lower, they started their journey back to the lodges. It was hot, but the big leaves sheltered them from the direct heat of the sun. Silently, they followed the path one after another like ants building their city.

Saving their energy to make the final path home like the sloth.

Following their way, despite any obstacle, like the river.

And following the light of the sun like the trees.

She had come to the island, escaping her life. But what she found was something deeper.

Belonging. To the world. To herself.

Not by rushing. Not by conquering. But by being open to the wonders of the world.

To ants.

To sloths.

To trees.

To the river.

To strangers.

To new paths.

They finally arrived exhausted but fulfilled with achievement, joy, and a sense of completeness. They hugged each other to say goodbye.

Gregg looked her in the eyes and said:

"Funny, isn't it? So many come here on vacation to get away from everything, but the truth is they are coming home." She couldn't quite understand what he meant. She was too tired from the hike.

This night she slept profoundly. She felt the jungle had wrapped her in its arms. She dreamt that the trees turned into living creatures, and the biggest one was whispering into her ear: *Careful, Maya. This island has a habit of waking up the parts of you you've been too busy to meet. But no worries. You're not becoming someone new out here, Maya. You're just starting to remember who you were before others told you to be somebody else.*

21

FOLLOW THE RED FROG

The sun had barely kissed the tops of the trees when Maya stepped out of her lodge, barefoot and quiet the next morning. Gregg's words were still echoing in her chest:

"So many come here on vacation to get away from everything, but the truth is they are coming home." And then, the dream of the talking tree. She tried to remember what it had said: *"You're not becoming someone new. You're remembering who you are."* What was that all about? She hadn't fully processed it. But something had shifted. Something had cracked open. And this morning she needed space to let it land.

She got dressed, packed her diary into her backpack, and left her lodge. The big house was still half-asleep in the early light. Nobody else was up.

She followed the path she now knew. The one that had once felt foreign and wild. The one where she'd stumbled and fallen just days ago. How clumsy she'd been. How cautious. Today, her feet moved easily over the stones and roots, her body weaving through the trees with quiet confidence. The jungle no longer challenged her. It welcomed her like an old friend.

Then something moved quickly in front of her. A flash of red jumped from one puddle to another. It was a frog. It was not green, but red. Fiery. As if it had been dipped in sunset. Maya froze. Back home, frogs were different. Ordinary. Expected. But this one? This one was a surprise she hadn't seen coming. It didn't croak or hop again. It just stared at her for a long moment, as if it knew something she didn't yet understand. Like it wanted to tell her something.

What message could it hold? she wondered.

Is there beauty in standing out?

That whatever coat you wear, what's underneath remains the same?

That the world still hold surprises, even on familiar paths?

She smiled softly, nodded at the tiny creature, and kept walking. Each step after that felt more awake. More intentional. She wasn't just retracing steps. She was walking toward something. As she stepped onto the beach, the world opened up before her. The ocean on the palm beach looked somehow like the picture in the social media post she saw when she booked it. But it was more profound. Deeper. A feeling no picture could describe.

The waves rolled in their rhythm, steadfast and unbothered by time. The sand was cool beneath her feet. The air was salty and soft. The shipwreck stood still in the distance, beautiful in its own strange way. Once broken, now a landmark for her. A compass. A reminder that a ruin could also be a kind of becoming. Seagulls soared above her, gliding wide arcs in the sky, unhurried and observant. From up there, they could see everything. The whole jungle. The whole shore. The whole journey.

A different perspective, she thought.

She found a spot near the edge of the beach, where the palm leaves sheltered her from the sun and the breeze carried the ocean's breath. She took out her diary. She hadn't written down her thoughts in ages. But now, it felt like the only thing she could do. For a long while, she just stared at the page. Listening. Feeling. Then, she wrote. Not what she did or what she wanted to be. But who she was.

Who am I?

I am not what you think I am.

I am not my CV.

I am not my calendar.

I am not their expectations.

I am not the title I chased.

Not the versions of me I built to be accepted.

Not the mask I wore to survive in rooms that never felt like mine.

I am not performance.

Not productivity.

Not perfection.

I am the girl who used to sing out loud in the car with the windows down.

I am the friend who remembers birthdays, but forgets to celebrate her own wins.

I am messy like my hair.

I am silence that listens.

I am softness not as weakness, but as quiet power.

I am barefoot on unfamiliar soil, finally starting to trust my steps.

I am the one who craves deep conversations and silly jokes,

who wants to feel needed, but not owned.

Seen but not defined.

Free but not alone.

The girl who once believed life was meant to feel like play.

The woman who now knows that joy is sacred,

and joy is not a luxury.

It's her birthright.

She stopped writing, her hand trembling ever so slightly. The words that had just poured out of her now stared back. Raw, unfinished, and real. It hit her like a warm wind across the skin. Not all at once, but in waves. Memories that rose from the ocean of her past. There were times when she was that vibrant, laughing being. Not broken. Not burnt out.

She remembered the long family car rides, years ago. The windows were rolled down with her sister beside her. They were both singing their hearts out to their favorite rock songs with no shame and no filters. Their voices were completely off-key and wild, shouting lyrics into the wind. Her parents played their own "radio show" from the front seats. Dad is doing dramatic voice-overs, and mom is adding jingles and commentaries as if the whole car were one giant, rolling joy machine. The world outside flew by, but inside, it was a music box full of laughter and love. Now she goes on vacation alone without her music box.

She remembered all the birthday parties she attended with all her excitement. She used to love creating birthday cards. She spent hours drawing, coloring, and finding just the right words. Picking the perfect present for each of her girlfriends wasn't a task; it was an act of care for her. She wanted her friends to feel seen, chosen, and special. It made her happy. Today, she writes a quick note on WhatsApp with no time to pick a present and celebrate.

She remembered the time with Ethan. Maya could still feel the warm hush of their old apartment in the evening, the clink of wine glasses, the glow of candles, and soft music playing in the background. They would talk for hours about dreams, setbacks, and silly things they read that week. She loved how he opened up to her, how he spoke like he trusted her with everything. And then, somewhere between the laughter and the quiet, the words would stop. They would drift closer, inch by inch, and kiss slowly, tenderly until silence turned into touch. The way he held her, how her body curved perfectly into his, like a puzzle piece finally in place. That kind of closeness was rare. And once, it had been hers.

She remembered her first months at the new job when it still felt like an excitement instead of a prison. How proud she'd been when they offered her the role. She had slowly earned their trust. There were real conversations back then with lunchtime debates, deep talks about purpose, and silly jokes scribbled on sticky notes left on each other's desks. At that moment, it felt like a team. Like belonging.

She used to love her own company. To curl up in a corner with a good book and disappear for hours, immersing herself in fictional stories. She would run along the river or do yoga at sunrise, feeling every stretch, every breath, like a quiet celebration of being alive. Those were the moments she felt most grounded when it was just her, her body, her mind, and the steady rhythm of her breath.

She had lived. There had been so much joy. So much aliveness. And somehow she had lost it. Not in one blow, but in a thousand small ways. In trying to fit into a mold too tight for her spirit. In chasing perfection in a world that only applauded performance.

In wearing a mask in fear of being rejected otherwise. In surviving the city jungle, where sharp elbows earned more than open hearts. She had traded laughter for efficiency. Connection for control. Presence for performance. And somewhere along the way, the light had dimmed.

But now, now that the memories came alive again in her chest, she realized something with a gentle ache: That girl, that woman, that Maya, she wasn't gone. She had just been waiting. Waiting for Maya to remember. And finally, she did.

She looked out at the sea, the waves continuing their eternal rhythm. The red frog appeared in her mind again, that brief flicker of wild color in a green world. Maybe that was her, too. Not here to blend in and adapt. But to wake up. To stand out in her own truth. She closed the notebook and whispered into the wind,

"I remember now."

She looked out into the ocean and said:

"Thank you for getting me this far. I'll take it from here."

22

UNTANGLED

Maya had spent hours just listening to the waves, soaking in the sunlight, and simply being. Her thoughts were quiet for once. She used to equate stillness with danger. Now it felt like safety.

Eventually, her body asked to move. Not with urgency. Not toward anything specific. Just forward. So she started walking along the beach. The day was luminous, the sky was painted in soft blues, and the seagulls were soaring effortlessly in lazy spirals above her. The waves crashed rhythmically against the shore, and the white sand shimmered like crushed pearls beneath her bare feet. Here and there, a few tourists lingered under palm shadows, sipping from coconuts, and were lost in their own world of paradise.

She passed the stand of the coconuts. The coconut lady was arranging her cart in her usual happy way, humming that same warming melody. The woman gave Maya a knowing nod, eyes twinkling as if she already sensed where this journey might lead. There was something about her presence, rooted, soft, and joyful, that lingered in the air like incense.

Maya smiled. She felt it too.

The silhouette of a small village emerged. She saw rooftops and stalls. Despite the sound of the ocean, she could hear the faint clinking of pots and murmured voices. The memory of the market came rushing back, vibrant and sensory-rich. She remembered the colors, the chaos, and her being completely in awe.

But it wasn't where her feet were leading her. Around a bend of jagged rock where the beach narrowed and the palms grew dense, she reached a small fisherman's cove. Wooden boats were scattered on the sand like sleeping animals. Nets were draped across them like blankets.

And then she heard it. Shouting. Not angry. Not panicking. But sharp and urgent. She picked up her pace. As she rounded the final curve, her breath hitched. A group of fishermen had formed a half-circle near the shoreline. Their hands moved quickly. Their voices were overlapping, and their bodies moved tensely. And in the center of them, caught and thrashing, she got a glimpse of a sea turtle. Not just any turtle. A giant, ancient-looking creature. Her shell was worn and wise, marked with the textures of time, of places crossed and storms endured. Her flippers beat helplessly against the sand, kicking up salt and foam. The turtle's energy was fading with each strike. It was wrapped tightly and suffocating in a thick snarl of green fishing net. It bound its legs, carved into its soft underbody, and even twisted around the mouth, leaving it unable to eat freely. Maya froze. The image struck something deep. Not just sympathy, but recognition. She almost could feel the pain the turtle must have. That tightness. That helplessness. Tangled.

One of the fishermen knelt beside the turtle, gently stroking

her head, murmuring calming words. Another tugged desperately at the net with bare hands. Maya snapped into action.

"Wait!" she called, breathless, already dropping to her knees.
"Wait! I think I can help."

They looked startled. One man raised an eyebrow. Another
simply stepped aside. Maya rummaged through her backpack
with shaking hands. There, tucked in a small side pouch, was
her manicure kit. It was her emergency "just in case" kit she
always carries with her. She opened it, pulled out a small, silver
pair of scissors. Ridiculous, she thought. These were made for
cuticles, not for a fisher's net. But they were all she had. She
held them up in triumph, ready to start the operation.

"Can someone hold her steady?" Not knowing if anyone
even understood her. A few men nodded. One placed his strong,
calloused hands gently on the turtle's shell, steadying her with
care. Maya leaned in. The net was like a second skin. Almost
soft in places. Familiar. Like a warm blanket turned prison.
Small bits of seaweed and fish clung to it like deceptive gifts.
False nourishment. A trap disguised as a bounty. She slid the
scissors carefully beneath the first strand. Snip. A sliver of
tension was released. Then another. Snip.

The turtle flinched, but Maya whispered, "It's okay. We got
this. You will be okay."

Piece by piece, fiber by fiber, she cut around the legs, around
the shell, and the mouth. It took time, patience, and focus, but
she didn't stop. The wet net eventually fell away in a heavy,
useless heap beside them. It was no longer a snare, just a lifeless
memory.

The turtle didn't move. For a breathless moment, Maya
thought they were too late.

Suddenly, she saw a flicker, a slow stretch of a flipper, and

116

then another. Her mouth opened once. Twice. And then, as if remembering she was free, she pushed forward. The fishermen stepped back reverently.

The turtle crawled toward the water with aching grace, dragging behind her the weight of freedom. The waves met her like an old friend. She stepped inside. And just like that, she was gone. The ocean welcomed her back and had taken her home again.

Maya sat back. She was soaked and speechless. The men around her murmured in awe. One placed a hand over his heart, another gave a small bow, some clapped, one hugged another, and all of them smiled at her. She smiled back. There was no need for words. The feeling of gratitude, humility, and relief spoke louder than anything else.

The fishermen returned to their work, as if nothing had happened. As if saving a turtle in the middle of the day was just part of their daily routine.

Maya remained on the sand, still in shock at what had just happened. She felt exhausted. She stared at the discarded net.

How did the turtle get caught in it in the first place? Maybe she was lured by the tiny fish still tangled inside. Maybe it looked like an easy meal. Maybe it felt warm, familiar, and safe. Maybe the turtle stayed longer than she should have because movement was still possible. And sometimes, it's easier to stay tangled than to risk swimming free.

The thought hit her hard. Maya had done the same. She remembered the job interview with Richard. It all sounded too good to be true. She was blinded by the great office, the free coffee, and the fruits on the table. The false friendliness of Richard. She felt safe once. The net hadn't looked like a trap at first. It looked like success with prizes hanging everywhere. Didn't Maya, by herself, hold on to titles, awards, and approvals? She felt a strange comfort in a busy calendar and a full inbox. It was the illusion of being needed and important. But it had wrapped itself around her little by little. Until she couldn't breathe anymore. She was tangled and in pain, just like the turtle.

She stood slowly, brushing sand from her legs. Her scissors were dull now, crusted with salt, but glinting in the sun like treasure. She tucked them back into her bag with care. As she walked back to her lodge along the beach, the tide curling around her ankles, she caught her reflection in the wet sand. She saw herself barefoot, wild-haired, and sun-kissed. Different.

She just helped to free another life. A mirror of herself, untangling her own life.

But it had left her with one question:

What would it feel like...

To swim free?

23

THE STORIES WE CARRY

The island was glowing in that golden hour way, soft and honey-warm, like it was holding its breath. Maya approached the Nature Lodges. She was barefoot and still covered in sand and seaweed. A scent of fish smell was still clinging to her from the encounter with the turtle. The day had carved something into her. She was nearly back at her lodge when she heard her name.

"Maya!" She turned.

It was Maria. She was barefoot too. Her hair was piled high on her head. She was holding a bowl of something that smelled like grilled pineapple and spice.

"We're lighting the fire tonight," Maria said, smiling.

"Last night, for a few guests. Come join us. It's tradition."

Maya hesitated for a breath. Then nodded.

She took a quick shower, washing off the salt and sand but keeping the wildness. Some things, she didn't want to lose.

By the time she returned, the fire was already crackling in front of the main house. The flames were dancing as if they knew they were being watched. Around it was a semicircle of mismatched chairs, floor cushions, driftwood logs, and scattered laughter. The smell of smoke and sweet spice curled through the air like a slow invitation.

At the heart of the gathering was Maria, its anchor. She stood beside a makeshift grill fashioned from an old oil drum. She held a pair of long wooden tongs in one hand and a marinated jackfruit skewer in the other. Her sarong was tied high on her waist, her hair wrapped in a loose scarf. Her curls were escaping in every direction. Smoke swirled around her like incense, and her face glowed from the firelight and the heat of the grill. Beads of sweat glistened on her brow as she moved with graceful certainty, turning sizzling fish, brushing glaze over plantains, and lifting grilled vegetables with a kind of reverence. She hummed softly, a melody without words, a lullaby that made the whole scene feel enchanted, like it belonged to another time.

The honeymoon couple sat curled together on a striped blanket, still wrapped in the sweet, awkward intimacy of new beginnings. She wore a flower in her hair. He rested his arm around her shoulders like he never wanted to let go.

The young family was there too. The parents gently guided their two little ones away from the flames, helping them build sandcastles just beyond the circle. Their laughter floated up like wind chimes on the breeze.

Leo stood talking to a young woman near the edge of the firelight, with his hands tucked in his pockets. His voice was low and warm.

Maya spotted a young man, looking like a surfer out of a movie, sitting cross-legged near the fire. Someone she hadn't seen before, but who looked like he'd arrived with a suitcase once and never found a reason to leave. A guitar rested in his lap. His sun-bleached hair flickering in the firelight. When he looked up. Their eyes met. He smiled at her. It was the kind of smile that said, *I see you.*

In that very moment, Gregg arrived, weaving through the crowd like a charismatic shadow, with two coconut cocktails in hand.

"I figured you'd need one," he said, handing her the drink with a wink. "It's island policy."

Maya's heart swelled. Gina's words echoed in her head. *Have some cocktails! Enjoy!*

This wasn't just a gathering. It was a constellation of the people who had silently been beside her, unknowingly, during her unraveling. People who had shared breakfast, a cooking session, a jungle trek, or simply a smile. Little kindnesses that added up to something big.

Someone offered to help Maria with the barbecue. She waved them off gently.

"This is my joy," she said, smiling without turning. "Let me feed you."

And she did with smoky flavors, with warmth, and with care as if everyone belonged to her as family. They ate with their hands the sticky, sweet, and smoky food. The fresh mango, grilled fish, and roasted breadfruit were delicious. They sipped from coconut shells and clinked bottles of local beer. Someone passed around a tray of homemade rum shots. Someone else passed a ukulele.

The fire popped. A hush settled. Maria stood with a spark in her eyes.

"Tonight," she said, "we tell stories."

A murmur of approval rippled through the circle like wind through the leaves.

"Real ones. Imagined ones. Funny, messy, life-changing ones. Anything goes.

This is the island's way."

Her eyes met Maya's as if she had known what Maya was going through.

And so it began.

In the beginning, a quiet pause filled the air like the whole group was catching its breath. Then the woman from the honeymoon couple leaned forward, adjusting the flower in her hair.

"We almost ended things before we got here," she admitted, her voice soft.

"But this island reminded us why we fell in love in the first place."

She glanced at her husband. They kissed. The group clapped gently, warmly.

Leo, surprisingly, joined in with a grin.

"I almost married someone in Thailand after three days," he said.

"She left me for a goat farmer. I stayed for the view until Gregg dragged me out."

The circle roared with laughter.

Then the father of the young family spoke, his little son clinging to his side.

"I lost my job a few months ago," he said.

"Now I build sandcastles instead of business plans. And maybe"

smiling at his kids, "...maybe that's all I need. That is what really matters to me."

The barefoot surfer looked up, strumming a soft chord on his guitar.

"I came for a one-month break. That was four years ago. I lost my luggage, my plan,

and eventually, my ego. Now I teach surfing and talk to the ocean more than to people."

Gregg lifted his coconut theatrically.

"I once ran bars in five countries," he said.

"Now I serve rum on an island where no one asks your last name.

I've never made less or felt richer."

They all laughed. Cups were raised. Cheers whispered.

And in that moment, Maya saw it clearly. Every person around the fire carried their own invisible weight, their own quiet turning points. Everyone had a story, not always spoken, but always shaping them. She was not alone.

And then, without planning to, Maya stood up. She didn't rehearse. She didn't overthink. She just let the firelight speak for her.

"I came here because I was tired," she said quietly. "Tired in a way that sleep couldn't fix. I thought I was chasing success. But really, I was tangled in noise, in meetings, messages, and expectations." She looked around. The circle was still and listening to her.

"The island slowed me down. The people. The ocean. Even the sloths," she smiled.

A soft chuckle went around the fire.

"I learned from the island. From nature. From silence. From the people here.

And today from a turtle." Her voice caught, just slightly.

"She was trapped in a net. Almost didn't make it. But we cut her free.

And I think, in helping her, I set something free in me, too."

Silence.

Then, a gentle applause came from the group.

The kind that wraps around you like a warm towel after a storm.

Maria raised her cup. "To Maya."

"To Maya," the circle echoed.

This wasn't just a dinner.

It was a ritual. A revelation.

And for some, a feast of endings.

And for some, a celebration of beginning.

24

THE SURFER WHO SPOKE IN WAVES

The island had grown quieter. Most of the guests had already left that morning. When Maya stepped into the main house, the silence was thick, almost sacred. The remains of last night's party still lingered. Empty coconuts lay scattered on the floor, cushions were tossed around like afterthoughts, and the fireplace cradled a soft bed of ash. It was a silent reminder of the bonfire they had all shared.

Funny, Maya thought. *You come together on a remote island and then, just like that, everyone goes their separate ways again. For a fleeting moment, it feels like you've known each other forever, and then a second later, you become strangers again.*

She didn't hear Maria's usual morning humming, nor the familiar clatter of pans in the kitchen. Maria was probably still asleep after last night's celebrations. The table had been lovingly set for breakfast. Maya sat down, poured herself a big cup of coffee, and took her time with toast and mango jam. She let the silence fill her up instead of scaring her as it normally did.

It was another warm, golden day. She decided to spend her last full day exactly where it all began on the beach. Now that she knew the way, she didn't hesitate. Her bare feet found the familiar trail, and as she reached the shore, her heart lifted. The sight of the waves, their gentle rhythm, calmed her. The sound soothed her soul. Seagulls circled above. Their chatter was playful and wild. She felt strangely accompanied and not alone. She sat down and let herself watch the ocean.

Out there, dancing on the waves like he belonged to them, was the lone surfer she had seen the first day. It looked so effortless, like he and the sea were made of the same breath. When he came out of the water, Maya's heart skipped. It looked like a TV advertisement, a man rising from the deep ocean. And then it hit her like a shock wave. It was him. The barefoot surfer with the guitar from the bonfire yesterday. He began walking toward her. Maya's pulse quickened.

Why am I nervous? she wondered.

He's just a surfer on a beach.

And I'm leaving tomorrow like every other tourist. Gone and forgotten.

He stopped right in front of her. His surfboard was tucked under one arm, the other hand resting calmly on his hip, like time had no claim on him. His wet hair clung to his face. He looked surprised, but his smile was warm and grounding. It was not the performative pick-up grin of city bars. It was this familiar smile again that said: *I see you.*

"Morning," he said. His voice was warm and rough like driftwood.

"Hey," Maya replied, cautiously and curiously. "You're out here often?"

He shrugged. "Yeah. The waves don't wait. They teach you

126

that."

He looked about her age, or maybe in his forties. She couldn't tell. His eyes held something rare: time. Not in years. In depth. Like he is truly living his moments, not rushing through them.

"I'm Gio, by the way."

"Oh, Maya." She smiled, realizing they hadn't even exchanged names last night.

"Mind if I sit and rest for a while with you?"

"Sure," she said, unsure why her voice sounded softer than usual.

He stuck his board in the sand. It stood beside them like a silent third presence.

He sat down beside her. They didn't speak at first. They just sat. Watching the waves. No urgency to fill the silence. No need to explain themselves. The stillness between them felt alive. Like something sacred. A connection without contact.

Then Maya tilted her head. "Can I ask you something?"

He nodded once, offering space without pressure.

"What are you doing here?" she asked. "You seem like someone who figured it out."

A soft laugh rumbled in his chest.

"I came here to run away," he admitted. "Burnt out. Years ago. Like you probably."

Maya blinked. "Was it that obvious?"

"Only to someone who's been there."

She looked out to the horizon. "Yeah. I was in pretty bad shape when I arrived."

He nodded. "I saw you at the shipwreck a few days ago. I was surfing out here.

You looked like someone carrying a heavy load."

And just like that, something inside her gave way.

The curtain lifted. She found herself telling him everything. About her toxic job. Her crumbling relationship. The mother who always expected more but gave so little. The loneliness. The numbness. The unhappiness. The way she had booked this trip on a whim, in desperate hope to escape a life she didn't enjoy anymore.

And Gio just listened. No interruptions. No advice. Just presence.

"I thought this trip would be the answer," she confessed.

"That I'd find some clarity on how to fix my situation and about what to do next.

But now..." Her eyes dropped to her hands.

"I'm not sure what I want and where to start."

The waves answered in rhythm, patient and steady.

"Have you ever tried watching a wave too closely?" he asked gently.

She looked up. "What do you mean?"

"If you try to analyze where it begins, where it'll crash, how tall or fast it will become,

it'll knock you over. Every single time." He paused.

"You have to ride it. Let go. Feel your way through."

She nodded. "You're saying I'm still trying to understand my life instead of just

feeling it."

"Exactly."

"But how do you know where to go?"

"You don't," he said simply.

"But you'll always know when you're going the wrong way. You will feel it."

Maya stared at him. "What do you mean?"

He smiled. "Your body knows. It always does. It tells you

when you are not okay. When your hands shake from coffee and panic, when your head hurts from overstimulation, when your stomach twists because there's something you can't digest, when your ears ring because there's too much noise and you can't hear your own voice anymore, when your knees tremble before an important speech because deep down, you think you don't belong."

Her breath caught. "That's me."

She thought of Richard's unrelenting demands, of the board members' curt dismissal, of her mother's disappointed tone, of Andrea's exhausted optimism, and Ethan's final words. And for a second, the world tilted. She was dizzy and wasn't sure if it was the sun or the truth. She was not okay. Her body had been trying to tell her all along.

Gio noticed. But he said nothing.

She steadied herself with a deep, purposeful breath. And then the memories of the last few days came back to her. Maria's wonderful presence, the lively market, the beautiful nature trail, the lovely coconut woman, and the breathtaking beach. Her body seemed fine here. She exhaled.

"I don't think I want my life back home anymore," she whispered.

Gio nodded, eyes scanning the horizon. "Then you simply won't go back."

Maya shrugged, and for a quick second, she imagined herself staying on this beach. Every day, a cocktail in one hand, barefoot and accompanied by laughter with Gio, who drops philosophy between sips of coconut water.

He chuckled, as if he were reading her mind.

"That's the life I chose four years ago. Since then, I knew that every single day is here to live it to the fullest. And if I die tomorrow surfing out there, I have lived it. And I am proud of that. I have no regrets. But it doesn't mean you have to live it. You might go back to the same place. But you can choose to NOT go back the same. You can choose to change."

She smiled.

"But what if I don't know what I want instead?"

"You don't need to," he said.

"Let the new you find you. She's on her way and will let you know."

That sounded strange to Maya, and she let those words sink in.

Silence fell again.

After a while, Gio stood, brushing the sand from his board.

"You know," he said, turning back to her, "most people think joy is a destination."

Maya looked up.

"But it's a choice. It is a wave you ride, not a shore you reach."

He winked. "And you, Maya, you look like you're almost ready to stand on your

own board."

She grinned. "I don't even know how to surf."

"Then maybe," he said, stepping into the water, "you just haven't found your wave yet."

And with that, he paddled out, disappearing into the shimmer of the sun, leaving Maya behind, but fortunately for Maya, he did not get too far out of sight..

Will she ever be ready to ride her own wave?

25

THE NORTH STAR

Gio rode the next wave back to shore, and they spent the rest of the afternoon together, tucked into the rhythm of beach life. They had no plans, and their clocks were irrelevant. The time was just unfolding right in front of them. They ate grilled octopus with their fingers and juice from fresh mango dripping down their wrists. They bought coconuts from a boy no older than ten, who cracked them open like a magician. It was refreshing to live through the day without meetings, without rules, and make-up. It was just Maya. Just Gio. Just this day. At home, she used to function according to plan and fit in. She was terrified of being seen without make-up, real and vulnerable. Now she sits with someone who truly sees her, and she welcomes it.

Later in the afternoon, between bites and giggles, Gio convinced her to try surfing. And she tried. Oh, she really tried. Each wave tossed her off like a wild horse refusing to be tamed. She surfaced, coughing, hair tangled in her lashes.

"I am terrible at this."

"You're still analyzing it," Gio said,

watching her spit seawater from her mouth for the third time.

"You're trying to master it. Control it."

"You're thinking too much," he added from the shore, laughing.

"You're not supposed to understand the wave. You're supposed to feel it."

"I feel like drowning."

"You're not," he said calmly, wading toward her. "You're just starting."

She stared at him, water dripping from her chin. "That's not comforting."

He grinned, pulling her up again.

"Good. That means there's no pressure to be perfect."

And despite the tumbles, she found herself laughing more than she had in months. Even when she failed, and failed again, they had fun. The way he taught her wasn't technical. It wasn't strategic. It wasn't even particularly effective. But it was kind. She got more confident with time. And after hours of trying, she was able to stand on the surfing board for a couple of seconds before she got thrown over by the next wave again. She was proud of herself. Just for a second, she was riding a wave too.

When the sun began to lower itself toward the horizon, painting the sky in soft oranges and pinks, they collapsed onto their towels again, salty and breathless and full of joy. Its golden glow stretched across the water like a pathway to another world. Gio pointed toward a small hill of rocks.

"Come," he said. "Let's watch the sunset from the top."

They climbed barefoot, hand in hand, until they reached a quiet ledge that overlooked the sea. Maya gasped. The sun hung heavy and swollen on the edge of the horizon, casting hues of

132

fire and honey into the sky. The sea reflected it all like liquid glass. It wasn't just a sunset. It was a symphony of light. They sat down, shoulders barely touching, and watched in silence.

"This never gets old," Gio whispered.

"No," Maya said. "It's like the world is exhaling."

She hadn't realized she'd been holding her breath until she let it go.

When the last sliver of gold melted into the water, Gio turned to her.

"Want to see something more sacred?" She nodded.

He led her down a narrow path to a smaller cove, sheltered by rocks and wild trees. The waves here whispered instead of roaring. The wind was softer. The sand cooler.

"Sit," he said. "Here. Close your eyes."

She sat cross-legged in the sand, still damp from the sea.

"Breathe in through your nose... slowly. Let your belly fill with air. Then exhale,

longer than your inhale."

She followed his rhythm.

"Again." And again.

With each breath, her mind let go a little more.

With each exhale, something inside her softened.

"This," he whispered, "is where you begin to hear yourself again.

Beneath the noise. Beneath the pressure. Beneath the roles and the titles."

The breath wasn't just air anymore.

It was permission. It was presence.

When she opened her eyes again, the sky had turned violet, scattered with the first

few brave stars.

"Look there," Gio said, pointing up. "That one. See it?"

"The brightest?"

He nodded. "That's Polaris. The North Star."

She stared at it, transfixed.

"It's been guiding travelers for centuries," he said.

"Sailors. Explorers. Nomads. They didn't have maps or GPS. Just that one light in the

sky. No matter where they were with storm, fog, or at night. It always showed

them where the north was. Where home was."

"What's your North Star, Maya?" he asked gently.

"What guides you when everything else is dark?"

Maya's throat tightened. She didn't have an answer.

"Even when everything around you changes," he continued,

"Even when you're lost, if you can find your North Star, you're never really drifting."

She was quiet for a long moment.

Then, softly she answered, "I don't think I ever had one."

Gio didn't say anything. He just sat still.

She looked at the star again. It was glowing and still.

"I used to think it was success," she whispered.

"Achievement. The next promotion. The title. The awards. The applause."

"And now?"

Now, it felt absurd.

"My North Star is joy," she said suddenly.

"It's laughter with no expectation. It's showing up messy and barefoot and being seen anyway. It's feeling alive without having to prove anything. It's being true to myself. Not what others expect. Not what makes them clap. I want to live without armor. I want mornings without dread. Work that doesn't feel like a slow drowning. I want a connection. Real connection. With others. With myself."

Her voice cracked.

"I want to feel happy in my own skin."

She looked at Gio, eyes wet, unblinking. "That's my North Star."

And in the quiet that followed, it didn't feel like a confession. It felt like a promise.

Gio reached out, his hand finding hers.

"That," he said, "is a beautiful direction."

They stayed there, side by side, under the blanket of stars. The waves moved like breath. The wind carried no answers, only presence. Maya had come to this island thinking she needed to escape. But here, in the stillness, she realized what she had needed was to return.

To herself.

To the truth she'd buried under ambition.

To the light she hadn't known she had lost.

And now?

She had found it again.

Not in a promotion.

Not in a five-step plan.

Not in someone else's approval.

But in her breath.

In the night.

In the quiet knowing.

The stars above shimmered silently.

And somewhere deep inside,

Maya began to shine, too.

26

LEAVING, BUT NOT LOST

The sound of birdsong stirred Maya from sleep, but this morning it didn't feel like a melody. It felt like a farewell. Golden light streamed through the window of her lodge again, catching on dust motes and dancing across the wooden floor like quiet memories. Her suitcase lay open at the foot of the bed. Half full. Half ready.

Maya wasn't even half ready to leave. She hadn't moved for almost twenty minutes. Her hands rested gently on her thighs, her breath slow, her heart tender. She was calm on the surface, but beneath, a current of something deeper stirred: fear, disbelief, and a quiet ache of love.

Last night still clung to her skin like salt. Gio's voice. His presence. His hand in hers as the stars whispered above them, and the sea hummed below.

His question echoed still, like a bell gently tolling in her chest: "What is your North Star?"

She had answered from her mind, but from her heart. And he hadn't tried to fix her. Hadn't tried to shape her next move.

He had simply held space. And her. That was the kind of love she hadn't known she needed. The kind that doesn't ask for a promise, only presence. That doesn't demand a future, but fully honors the now.

And this morning? He was gone. No knock. No note. No trace outside. Only the echo of his kiss on her cheek. A silent goodbye, pressed gently to her skin like a seal. A 'Thank you'. A 'You'll be okay'. A 'Maybe in another life'. She exhaled softly, finished packing, and zipped her suitcase with a finality that echoed through the quiet lodge.

Outside, the jungle shimmered in morning mist, tender and alive. The paths she once feared now looked inviting and familiar, like veins of the island. Something drew her to go down the path once more before she left. She followed it. Her flip-flops brushed the gravel, and the morning sun was warming her shoulders. She didn't go to the front of the main house to leave her keys. Not yet. She needed to say goodbye to the sea.

When she stepped out of the jungle and onto the sand, she almost didn't see him.

But there he was. Gio. Leaning against a tree, and arms crossed loosely over his chest. His surfboard was propped beside him. He was still barefoot and still wet from the ocean. As if he had come straight from the waves to say what words never could. Their eyes met. And at that moment, she couldn't breathe. Not because she was surprised he was there, but because a part of her had hoped he would be there. And now that he stood there, real, sun-kissed, waiting, her heart didn't know what to do with the flood of feeling. He walked toward her slowly. No rush. No words. No performance. Just truth in motion. When he reached her, he stopped. They stood face to face, close enough to feel the heat between them. The morning light bathed them in gold, like the island wanted to remember them this way. Neither of them spoke. Gio looked at her the way people look at sunsets, they know won't last but still choose to marvel at them anyway. His gaze held the kind of love that doesn't try to hold you but sees you clearly enough to make you want to stay. He reached out and gently tucked a strand of hair behind her ear. His fingers lingered just long enough to say *I was here*.

"I knew you'd leave lighter," he said, voice low, rough like driftwood.

Maya swallowed past the lump in her throat.

"I don't know what this is."

He shook his head softly. "You don't have to."

His hand found hers. And they stood in stillness.

"I'm not ready to go," she whispered.

He brushed a tear from her cheek, reverently.

"But you're ready to live," he replied.

"I am afraid to go back. I am afraid I will fall into my routine back home again.

I am afraid to forget the joy I once felt on this island."

Gio leaned closer to her. "The fact that you are afraid means you care.

Your intentions are good. That is all that matters.

Smile, breathe, and just be happy whatever you do."

"I am afraid I can't."

"You think you can't. But the truth is, you can. You are afraid to produce your

most important dream because you feel you don't deserve it, or you are unable

to achieve it. You think you are not ready, but you are."

139

He leaned in even closer and pressed his forehead to hers.

"Listen to your heart. Where your heart is, you will find your joy.

Keep listening to what it has to say."

They stood brow to brow, breath to breath. Hearts meeting in the quiet between beats.

No promises. No expectations. Only presence.

"Always remember, you are worthy of all the joy in the world. You are enough to receive it. And you are loved."

He pulled back just enough to kiss her, not on the lips, but on her heart.

His palm rested there, warm and steady.

"I'll be with you along the way," he said softly.

"In the pause. In the breath. Every time you choose joy, claiming your life you deserve."

She closed her eyes. Let it land. Let it root.

When she opened them again, he was already stepping back.

And she let him. Because loving him didn't mean keeping him. It meant feeling everything and still choosing to go. It was that kind of love without claiming ownership. He was never the destination. He was her compass. A signal that pointed her home.

Gio smiled at her once more. Then, without a word, he turned, picked up his surfboard, and walked toward the sea. And just like that, he was gone again. Riding the next wave.

Maya stood there for a long moment. Smiling through her tears. Then turned and walked back to the lodges.

When she reached the main house, she stopped. Maria was already there waiting. Not humming. Not bustling. Just standing in the doorway, her cotton dress swaying in the breeze, eyes soft and knowing. Like she had felt it all from a distance.

Without a word, Maria stepped forward and wrapped Maya in a big hug. This time it didn't feel uncomfortable. It was just what she needed. They held each other for a long moment. Two women. Two lives. One understanding. When they pulled apart, Maria pressed something into Maya's hand. It was a hand-carved wooden butterfly. His paint was in brilliant blue, and the wings were wide open, ready to fly. It looked just like the one in her lodge.

"For home," Maria whispered.

"For the days when the noise returns. Let this remind you of the quiet inside you.

The joy you are seeking. The wonder you are!"

Maya blinked back the tears.

"Thank you for everything."

Her voice was small and full of awe.

Maria smiled, her hand resting on Maya's cheek.

"You came crawling," she said. "You leave ready to fly."

Maya nodded. She turned to look back at her lodge. The place where she had fallen apart, and came alive. Then she tucked the butterfly safely into her bag, picked up her suitcase, and began walking down the gravel path for the last time. Maria stayed at the edge of the house, waving gently. Birds sang above her. The jungle rustled. The breeze tugged at her hair one last time like a blessing.

And Maya?

Maya didn't look back again.

Because she knew...

The island wasn't behind her.

It was within her now.

27

DEPARTURE

The drive to the airport was a blur. Not because Maya wasn't paying attention but because the scenery outside the window felt unreal like watching a movie in slow motion. The jungle slipped away behind her. The ocean waved its last goodbye. Even the potholes felt sacred, as if the island was doing its best to hold her just a little longer.

By the time she stepped into the open hallway of the airport, it felt like she had landed on a different planet. Tourists were everywhere again. Busy. Hustling. Buying their last souvenir. Ready to go back. Maya was not.

This was limbo. A space suspended between stories.

Her flip-flops echoed quietly as she walked with her backpack over one shoulder. Her butterfly from Maria was safely tucked inside. She dragged her big suitcase behind her, and her clothes still smelled faintly of woodsmoke and mango. Her skin was sun-kissed. Her heart? Still vibrating from everything it had held.

She stood in line with sunburned tourists and chatty families. Their energy was buzzing with return flights, timelines, and what 's-for-dinner-tonight. She nodded politely. But she wasn't really here.

When the check-in clerk asked the usual questions, Maya answered on autopilot.

She was elsewhere. Not ready to leave.

Once checked in, she found a quiet corner by a window. Planes blinked outside in the distance. She sat cross-legged and opened her diary. It was the same one that had gathered fragments of this journey.

She read through her last writing about who she was again. So much has happened since she arrived here eight days ago. She took a pen and began to write again as if keeping her memory alive, as if she wanted to catch the moments to never forget and carry them everywhere she goes.

She wrote.

Day 1
Arrival.
The rain came down in sheets.
I couldn't see the road. Couldn't feel my feet.
Everything was soaked, loud, unfamiliar, and chaotic.
I was scared, lost, tired, and exhausted.
Almost turned back out of fear, helplessness, and doubt.
But I didn't. I made it. (Now looking back, I am glad I stayed.)

Day 2
The jungle path. My first fall.
I slipped into thick mud and for the first time in a long time,

I laughed.

Not a performance. A real, belly-deep laugh.

That moment stripped me of my polished exterior.

It reminded me how much I clung to control.

That day, I began to *let go*.

Day 3

The shipwreck.

A broken boat buried in sand, hollowed by time.

I saw myself in that forgotten shell, drained, rusted, and quietly aching.

But that day, the ocean helped me to release my negative emotions.

It's okay to break apart. That's how new shapes begin.

The coconut lady.

Old, joyful, utterly content.

No growth plan. No hustle. Just enough.

She looked me in the eye and said everything without words.

And I wondered:

What if I stopped building empires and just built joy?

Day 4

The market.

Sensory overload. Chaos, colors, noise, spices, heat.

Everything is pulsing with life.

And for once, I didn't run from the overwhelm.

I was open to it. Curious.

I stopped trying to fit it into my boxes.

I accepted it and moved along.

Maria.

She taught me how to cook.

No recipes. No measurements. Just taste, instinct, and laughter.

Fed me like a mother. Hugged me like a sister.

Held space like a wise woman who had done this a thousand times before.

Her food nourished more than my body.

Between the spices and stories, the silence and smoke

I remembered how to nourish myself again.

Day 5

The hike with Gregg and Leo.

Nature taught me so much.

The ants showed me that working together, we can achieve greatness.

The trees don't grow in a rush; they reach the light anyway.

The sloth reminded me that energy is sacred and to use it only where it truly matters.

The river always finds a way, no matter what obstacle is in its way.

No matter what stood in our path, rocks, roots, ferns,

We didn't stop either.

We didn't follow a beaten path, we followed our own.

Day 6

The turtle.

She was caught in the net. She was panicking and exhausted.

We freed her. Slowly. Gently. One thread at a time.

And as she crawled back to the sea,

I realized I'd been tangled too

in expectations, roles, and stories that weren't mine.

That day, I didn't just set her free, I set myself free, too.

The bonfire.

One flame. Many stories.

People shedding their truths like old skin.

No filters. No pretending.

And I found myself doing the same.

I spoke about my fear, my numbness, and my burnout.

And instead of judgment, I was held by a community.

We all carry pain. We are not alone.

Day 7

Gio.

He didn't hand me answers.

He handed me a surfboard. I was terrified.

He did not save me. He reminded me that I am safe already.

"Stop analyzing the wave," he said.

"Feel it."

Life isn't about mastering the ocean but learning how to ride it.

The North Star.

Sitting with Gio, under the magical sky.

He asked me what guided me.

It took me a long time to answer.

And I finally said it, not as a slogan, not as a pitch right from my heart.

joy.

Day 8

The goodbye.

I was afraid to leave. I was afraid to forget.

But Gio reminded me: what lives in your heart can't be lost.

He did not ask me to stay. He asked me to keep going.

And that was love.

Maria's gift, a blue butterfly, shall always anchor the truth deep within me.

I am magical. Ready to fly.

Maya was jolted from her thoughts by a sudden, loud voice. The final boarding call echoed overhead. She closed her diary and put it into her bag. She stood and walked to the gate. The airline agent smiled and handed her the boarding pass.

"Have a safe trip," he said.

Maya looked down at it. It read: Return. But Maya knew better. She wasn't returning. She was arriving at a new way of being. The island would stay with her. In a way, she experienced a new environment not as danger, but as a treasure to be uncovered. In the way she saw strangers not as threats, but as stories waiting to be heard. In a way, she discovered nature not as a mere existence, but as true wonder. In the way she started her mornings with a deep breath of peace instead of panic, survival mode. In the way she went through the day, not as dragging but full of joy. She entered the airplane and sat down in her seat. Then tucked her bag beneath it while her fingers were brushing against the wooden butterfly Maria had given her that morning.

The cocoon had opened.

She was ready to fly.

III

THE RISE

"Let the beauty of what you love
be what you do."
Rumi

28

THE RETURN

The plane touched down with a thud, jolting Maya from the edge of sleep. Her body tensed instinctively, the way it always did at the end of a journey, as if bracing for re-entry into a world that moved too fast.

Outside the window, the landscape blinked past in gray and glass, in concrete and speed. Runways crisscrossed, and airport lights flickered like impatient eyes. The city wasn't cruel. But it was unrelenting. A rhythm of motion she once called home.

The seat belt sign went off, and passengers immediately sprang to their feet like racehorses at the gate, elbowing into the aisle, yanking bags from overhead bins with the urgency of people trying to outrun their exhaustion. Phones were taken out and connected to the outer world. The woman right beside her had the phone glued to her ear, already telling the person on the other line that she had landed.

Maya remained in her seat, watching it all like a scene from someone else's life. For a moment, she let them go ahead. She didn't need to rush. Not this time. The city would still be there when she stepped off the plane, loud, bright, and impatient. But she decided she would step into it differently. And that made all the difference.

The taxi ride home felt like watching her old life on mute. Glass towers flashed past her window, monuments to ambition and sleepless nights. But instead of feeling trapped by them, she saw them for what they were, just buildings. No longer gods, no longer cages. Just structures. As they entered the city, the high-rises stood tall like majestic powerhouses, but today, Maya didn't flinch. They didn't tower over her. They simply stood. She could appreciate their symmetry now, the way their windows caught the morning sun and reflected it in fractured gold.

She felt the familiar buzz of urgency in the streets. The electric hum of a city that was always moving, but it didn't rattle her anymore. It was a rhythm she could choose to dance with or step away from. People rushed by with their heads down, clutching their coffee like shields, and for the first time, she didn't judge them. She just saw them. Beautiful, tired, driven humans, each with a story. Each, maybe, looking for their own way home.

Her office came into view. Still proud. Still sterile. But somehow it was smaller than she remembered. She didn't feel like a prisoner anymore. She felt like it was equal. If anything, it looked like it needed a soul. And for a fleeting moment, Maya wondered: *What if I brought mine back in?*

They passed her favorite cafe. It was still crowded, still loud, and still a caffeine-fueled chaos. But even that held a strange warmth. The comfort of routine, the quiet rituals that tether people to their mornings. The clinking of cups. The barista's grin. The familiar fog on the windows. It was messy and alive.

Outside, the air still had a winter bite, but spring was arriving. The sunlight streamed between buildings, soft and golden, stretching long across the pavement like a silent invitation: *Notice me.*

Maya did. She noticed it all. The city hadn't changed. But she had. And because of that, everything looked a little more beautiful. She looked down at her phone. Airplane mode was still on. Her thumb hovered over the WI-Fi button. She was hesitating. She wasn't ready. Not for the avalanche of emails, voicemails, and news. Not for the hamster wheel to start spinning again. But she couldn't live on her dream island forever. Eventually, she'd have to face reality. So, with a breath both soft and steady, she gave herself a gentle push and switched on the WI-Fi. The screen lit up instantly. 354 emails. 15 voicemails. 75 messages.

It all can wait. She thought.

She didn't even dare to check her social media. Not yet. Instead, she leaned her head against the window. Watched the streets roll by. Watched the people crossing on autopilot with their eyes down, phone in their hand, and rushing toward something they thought mattered.

The sun was shining. The air was lighter than she remembered. It was warmer than when she left. Spring has finally returned. And so had she.

She arrived at her apartment. Her building hadn't changed. She saw the same blinking security light when she entered, drove up the same elevator that groaned with age, and walked on the same familiar floorboards that creaked outside her apartment.

She turned the key. The door opened. Her apartment exhaled the breath it had held for eight days. It smelled like dust and something forgotten. The plants had surrendered. Her leaves were brown, wilted, and stiff like old bones. The laundry was still undone. A stack of unopened mail leaned against the wall like a disapproving parent. A chaos! Still here, waiting patiently. Her laptop, left on the kitchen counter, blinked awake beside a clutter of papers and plans. But she didn't stop. She didn't check.

She walked into the bedroom. Set her suitcase down gently and inhaled deeply. The air felt foreign. Or maybe she did.

She moved slowly and deliberately. Like every movement was a choice, not a reflex. She unpacked her suitcase in silence. Each item was placed not where it used to belong, but where it felt right now. She unfolded the dress she wore the night she found her North Star with Gio. She held it close for a moment as if she could recreate every moment of it here in her bedroom. She placed Maria's wooden butterfly gently on her bedside table. It looked just right with its wings wide, painted in blue, and catching the light from the window.

She slid her diary into the drawer, but not too deep. She knew she'd reach for it again soon. She lit a candle. Its flame flickered and danced like a familiar friend. Gratitude welled up in her chest. Gratitude for the quiet. For the lessons. For the island that had cracked her open and sewn her whole again.

She filled the kettle, listening to the soft gurgle as it began to boil. There was no rush. Nothing to chase. She made tea. She did not pick the instant kind she used to gulp between calls, she looked for the loose leaves. She poured the water over the leaves and carried the cup into the living room. She turned off the overhead lights and turned on the soft lamp by the window instead. She sat down on the couch with the tea cradled in her palms. The city blinked outside her window. Emails continued to flood. Voicemails kept piling up.

But Maya? Maya didn't move.

She watched the steam rise from her cup.

Watched the candlelight dance across the hardwood floor.

Watched herself in the window's reflection, barefaced, softer, quieter,

and somehow stronger.

She was not the woman who had left.

Not the one who packed panic in her carry-on.

Not the one who lived inside a fortress of unread emails.

Not the one who measured her worth by inboxes, likes, or perfectly

polished presentations.

That Maya had stayed behind somewhere between the jungle and the bonfire.

The Maya who returned?

She brought the island with her.

In the way she moved slowly.

In the way she saw the city with different eyes.

In the way she breathed, consciously.

In the way she refused to let the world dictate her first night back.

She reached for her diary, opened it to a fresh page, and wrote, in her calmest handwriting.

Let the world wait.

I just returned from the one that matters.

Then she closed the diary.

Blew out the candle.

And went to bed.

No alarms set.

No messages answered.

No apologies given.
Just sleep.
Just silence.
Just Maya.
Back home.
But not the same.

29

MAKING ROOM

The Sunday morning light crept in gently through the blinds, brushing the floorboards with warmth. Maya blinked awake. She had hoped to hear the birds outside, but instead she was accosted by the ceaseless hum of the city. When she opened her eyes, she was welcomed by her familiar apartment that emerged in chaos, rather than her little lodge immersed in the jungle. Her body was still wrapped in the slow rhythm of the island. When Maya entered her kitchen to get herself a coffee, she could still hear Maria singing in the back of her head.

Reality hit her harshly when she looked around her apartment. A mug with fossilized coffee was sticking to the TV table, the plant looked even more dead today than yesterday, and the wine bottle from her night of self-pity nine days ago was still on the floor. The laundry lay crumpled in corners, empty boxes that never got thrown away were scattered everywhere, and she found books on the floor that she didn't even remember buying or reading.

She sighed. This wasn't just a mess. It was her old life piled high, pressed into corners, filling the air like static, and her life with weight. She knew what to do. She rolled up her sleeves. Today was about cleaning up the mess. Today was about making space and clearing it for the life she wanted to let in.

She started with the living room. She cleaned up every corner, washed the dirty clothes, and dusted her shelves. She almost fainted from the smell opening the fridge. Out went the expired yogurt, the wilted lettuce, and the salsa from... she didn't want to know when.

She pulled down old company binders and books she had not touched for years, and the only purpose was to collect dust. Most of them landed in a donation box. She let herself be ruthless. If it didn't bring joy or at least a sigh of relief, it was gone. If she hadn't used it in the past twelve months, she decided to get rid of it.

By noon, the apartment already looked different. Clean. Liveable. And somehow empty.

She realized how wonderful her apartment was. It had all the comfort she needed. It was modern and luxurious. It had all the electronic gadgets, including the internet she was taking for granted. She felt privileged to live in such a wonderful place.

She had opened the windows to let the breeze in. It danced in the room like the island was saying, *Good job, love. Keep going.*

Later that afternoon, she grabbed her phone and called the one person who couldn't wait to hear back from her.

"Maya! You are back!" Gina, her best friend, screamed on the other line.

"I can't wait to hear all your stories!"

"Gina!" Maya beamed. "Come over."

Twenty minutes later, the doorbell rang just as Maya was stuffing the last donation bag by the door. She opened it to find

Gina standing there with a tote bag, wind-swept hair, and a look that could only be described as part relief, part drama.

"Okay," Gina said, stepping in without waiting, "What the actual hell happened to you?"

She dropped her tote and hugged Maya tightly.

"You disappear to a beach with no signal for over a week, and now I walk into this?"

She stood in front of a new Maya. Relaxed. Glowing. Sun-kissed.

Then she glanced around the spotless apartment, narrowing her eyes like it were evidence of a crime scene.

"Your apartment! No smell of stale coffee. No laundry mountain. And look at you!

You look stunning. No signs of emotional breakdown?

I don't know whether to be proud or deeply concerned."

Maya laughed. "Hello to you, too."

They sat down on the couch, a cup of lemongrass tea already waiting for them. Maya tucked her legs underneath and handed Gina a napkin with a still-warm muffin she'd picked up from the bakery downstairs.

"Okay, spill it!" Gina said between bites.

"Tell me what happened. Did you meet someone? Did you join a cult?

Was there a goat involved? You look too calm. I don't trust it."

Maya smiled, slowly.

"It's hard to explain. The island... it unraveled me. In the best way."

Gina blinked. "Unraveled? Girl, you left for eight days, not a decade."

"I know. But it felt longer. Everything was so different. I met other kinds of people.

I hiked barefoot through the jungle, learned a lot from nature, and met a woman

who sells coconuts with more wisdom than half the business books I've ever read.

I sat under the stars with a man who asked me what my North Star was."

Gina stared, mid-sip. "Okay. So... there was a man involved."

Maya rolled her eyes, smiling. "That's not the point."

"I mean, that's kind of the point," Gina teased. "But keep going. I'm listening."

Maya looked out the window for a second, choosing her words.

"I let go of a lot out there. Expectations. Pressure. This needs to always be 'on.'

I slowed down to hear my own voice for the first time in years."

Gina leaned back, sipping her tea. "That's what they call vacation, baby!"

Maya nodded.

"Now you are back! Life here is still loud, messy, and fast."

"It is. I'm not pretending it's not. But something shifted. I don't want to pick

everything back up the way I left it. I want less noise. More choice. More freedom.

More space to breathe. More joy. Not only on vacation but also here."

Gina was quiet for a beat.

Then: "You're serious, aren't you?"

"I am."

"I mean... I love that for you. Really. It sounds like you had a midlife awakening in

your summer dress and flip-flops on the beach under the palms while I was drowning

in deadlines and oat milk shortages."

They both laughed.

Gina smiled, softer now.

"Well, you do look stunning. And your place smells like lemongrass.

So whatever happened, it's working for now."

She squeezed Maya's hand.

"Just don't float away completely, okay? Some of us still need you here."

"I'm not floating away," Maya said.

She heard the voice of the old coconut woman in her head: *Be here, not there.*

"On the contrary. I am more present than ever." Maya replied.

Maya told Gina all her adventures in detail, and time just slipped away in between laughter, adoration, and gratitude. She was happy to be back enjoying her moments with her best friend. In the end, Maya also told her about Gio. Gina leaned in, eyes wide with curiosity.

"Okay, but seriously... tell me about him."

Maya smiled, soft and faraway.

"His name is Gio. He lives the life most people only dare to dream about."

She paused, then added quietly, "But the thing is, he's not just dreaming it. He's living it."

Gina blinked. "Damn. That's rare."

Later that evening, after Gina had gone with the leftover muffins, Maya sat by the window. The apartment was quieter.

Lighter. Clearer. There was space now. Space for new stories. There was room to breathe. Room to be. She curled up on the couch, candle flickering beside her, casting golden shadows on the walls.

The island was gone.

But what it had given her was right here.

Alive in silence.

Rooted in her.

30

THE SOUND OF THE SEA

Monday morning. 6:00 AM.

The alarm buzzed. But this time, it didn't drill into Maya's skull like a weapon. It simply... sang. A soft, familiar rhythm. A reminder that the world was moving again. And so was she. Her eyes fluttered open. She lay still for a moment, listening. The birds outside, which she had never heard before, were chirping. Not jungle birds this time, but city birds, the determined, scrappy, and urban survivors. It grounded her. She breathed in slowly and fully. Then smiled.

"Okay, world. Let's do this."

She did not press the snooze button this time. She rejected the inner war. She was ready for the day. The bed creaked softly as she sat up and stretched her arms toward the ceiling like she was reaching for the day itself.

The apartment was clean. The plants she'd bought yesterday were thriving and gave her a little sense of a lush, tiny jungle around her. The butterfly on the table shone in its beauty, like saying to her: *You have wings too.* The old furniture hadn't

163

magically changed, but it felt lighter. Or maybe she was.

She moved with grace to the kitchen to make her first coffee of the day. Her hands wrapped around her ceramic mug. It was her favorite one, handmade and slightly chipped. She took a sip. The coffee was strong. But she wasn't relying on it to survive today. It was just a warm friend, not a crutch. She felt content.

She looked outside the window. The city was still in a rush. Buses hissed. Horns barked. A sea of humans on autopilot. But Maya felt she was no longer swimming in it. She was walking beside it, barefoot in her mind.

She was taken out of her daydream by the buzzing of her phone. It was a new message. Probably another mail piling up on top of the hundreds she has received over the last week, or Andrea trying to reach her, or maybe even Richard barking at her again.

She had another sip of her coffee.

They can wait till my official office hours start.

Way too long she had been starting the day by reading all her emails, messages, and social media right when she woke up. She decided not to do that anymore.

She dressed not to impress, not for armor but in clothes that made her feel both rooted and free. She decided to wear a white soft shirt and loose trousers. She added a necklace with the small shell she bought at the market. A reminder.

On her way out, she looked in the mirror. She just smiled at herself. She didn't see the tired woman in her 30s with dark circles under her eyes, skin too pale, cheekbones too sharp, and drained. She looked at a woman still in her 30s, but sun-tanned, shiny, and full of energy, beginning the day.

"You're doing good," she whispered.

The elevator ride down didn't feel like a descent into battle.

It was just a ride.

Traffic was chaotic as expected, but she put on music in her car to make her feel good. She chose not to listen to another podcast to learn something today or another motivational talk to push harder.

Just pleasant music to enjoy the ride. She eventually tuned in, singing out loud as she used to with her sister when she was a child. She sang as loudly as she could with the windows down.

When she arrived at the office, Andrea was already waiting for her. Her eyes were wide with that same anxious loyalty Maya used to wear like perfume.

"Maya. I am so glad you are back. There has been so much going on. Last week ...."

It sounded all a blur to Maya, like an echo far away, while Andrea was continuing.

... and Richard asking for the numbers of the second quarter ..."

Maya held up a hand. Not dismissively. Gently. Kindly.

"Good morning, Andrea," she said.

"Let me put my bag down. Then we breathe. We will get a fresh cup of coffee.

And then you can tell me all about it. Deal?"

Andrea blinked. Then smiled. "Deal."

Maya walked through the hallway. Same walls. Same cold lights.

Same colleagues typing frantically.

But this time, she didn't feel small.

She didn't shrink.

She didn't brace herself.

She didn't rush and didn't feel the anxiety.

She felt she belonged to herself now.

She entered her office. Opened the windows to let the fresh air in for a moment.

She didn't open her computer first, but her diary, which was in her bag.

She wrote just one line.

Today, I choose joy.

She turned her computer on.

The emails were still a mess.

The messages still blinked.

Richard was still Richard.

But Maya?

Maya was no longer dancing to their beat.

She had her own rhythm now.

The one that sounded like the sea.

31

THE POWER WITHIN

Her first meeting was with Richard. Of course. He didn't even look up when she walked in.

"Close the door," he barked.

The door slammed behind her.

But inside Maya? Nothing slammed. She was surprised at herself. She didn't feel the fear or panic rising as she used to, nor that old reflex to over-explain or overachieve her way back into approval.

She sat down calmly with her spine upright.

"You've been gone ten days," Richard began, with his sharp voice enough to slice bread. "And while you were off suntanning yourself, we were here picking up your pieces."

Maya breathed in slowly like Gio had taught her on the island. Then exhaled smoothly and steadily.

"I imagine that has been challenging," she said evenly. "But I trust the team managed well."

He blinked and was thrown off by the absence of guilt.

"I expected a fully revised strategy on my desk by now."

"I can't promise that," Maya replied, calm as tea. "And I won't be able to deliver it today."

He leaned back in his chair, incredulous. "Excuse me?"

"This pace, this pressure, it doesn't work for me anymore," she said, gently but

firmly. "And I won't betray myself just to keep up appearances."

The silence between them stretched thin.

Maya didn't flinch. Didn't fidget. Didn't fill it. She just breathed.

"I'll still deliver," she added.

"But on terms that are healthy and realistic for me. That's how I do my best work."

Richard narrowed his eyes. "So now you get to make your own rules?"

She smiled softly and powerfully. "I'm not making them up. I'm remembering what

they should've been all along."

His mouth opened, but nothing came out. He was speechless. She stood, steady and deliberate.

"Our next meeting is in two days. Andrea already sent the invite. I'll present the revised strategy then." With those words, she stood up and walked out like a woman who knew her worth and didn't require a single nod of approval.

When the door slammed behind her, she leaned against the wall. She took a deep breath and closed her eyes for a moment to enjoy her victory. She had stood up against Richard and had stood by herself, saying NO when it was enough. She was proud of herself.

Back at her desk, Andrea looked up, eyes wide. "What just happened?"

Maya gave her a half-smile. "Nothing dramatic. Just a bit of clarity."

She opened her laptop, scanned her inbox, and for the first time in forever, she didn't tense at the sight of unread emails. She read through them calmly, one after another, answering them, delegating what wasn't hers to carry. Declined two back-to-back meetings with a simple:

Not available at that time.

She gave no apology, nor justification. At exactly 5:00 pm, she closed her laptop. She closed it like a full stop, not a pause.

"Heading out," she said.

Andrea blinked. "But... there's still..."

"I know." Maya slipped into her coat. "And it'll still be there tomorrow."

Andrea watched her go, stunned. "You're... different."

Maya paused at the elevator. Turned.

"Not different," she said. "Better. Not faster. Not harder. Just... better."

That evening, there was no networking event, no extra hour of "just one more email.", no doom scrolling on social media wondering who had landed the next title, trophy, or TED talk.

Instead, Maya went for a walk. She did not want to get somewhere or achieve something. She did not have a plan. She just felt like going on a walk like that jungle hike with Gregg and Leo. Only now, the path was paved in asphalt, not mud, the vines were replaced by power lines, and the canopy above her was made of steel and glass, reaching for the sky like modern trees. She wandered aimlessly, letting the current of life move around her. The streets pulsed with urgency. People flowed past in fast-moving streams, heads down, phones up, and rushing somewhere like ants on a mission.

Maya didn't rush. She noticed things instead. The way a breeze slipped between buildings was like a secret. The way the late sunlight caught on the windows and scattered into soft patterns on the sidewalk. The scent of roasted chestnuts from a street cart. She had forgotten how much she loved the city.

She paused at a crosswalk, watching a pigeon hobble across like it owned the road. She laughed out loud. Nobody noticed.

She kept walking. A small bookstore appeared, tucked between two glowing chain stores. She hadn't seen it before, or maybe she never looked. In its window, a sign written in fading chalk: *You're not lost. You're just on a path you don't know yet.* Maya smiled. That sounded about right. She entered and looked around. She hadn't read a book in ages. That was about to change. She left the bookstore with a book in her hand, a quiet smile, and a spark of joy, already imagining the comfort of her couch and the thrill of getting lost in a new story.

She stopped at a small coffee shop not because she had to, but because the smell reached out and wrapped around her like a memory. Inside, she didn't scroll her phone nor planned her next move. She just sat there and observed. She ordered a cappuccino and spotted an old woman stirring her tea so slowly it brought back a memory. Maya smiled. *She might've been a sloth in a past life. Saving her energy for what matters.*

And there, in the middle of all that concrete, all that noise, all that motion, she felt still.

She was redefining herself.

No more worshipping hustle.

No more confusing burnout with value.

She was done betraying herself to please people who never even noticed the cost.

And with that small decision, she had never felt more powerful.

She paid for her cappuccino, stood up, and walked back home. She felt rooted and alive, like she had brought the island back, not in her suitcase but in every single step she was taking.

32

TAMING THE DRAGONS

Days flew by. But they didn't consume her. Maya was back. Not in the way she once was frazzled, over-caffeinated, juggling deadlines like ticking bombs. No. This time, she moved through her days with a different rhythm, a different vibe.

She still answered emails and still joined meetings, but she no longer gave away pieces of herself just to keep up appearances. She was clear about her boundaries. Clear about what she could do and what she could not. She was direct in her answers. She was surprised by herself at how easy it was to actually say no, and it seemed people respected her even more because of it. She stayed above the noise and actually enjoyed it.

Richard had accepted the new strategy she presented to him last week and had put it on the next board meeting agenda right away. She had rewritten the strategy. But more than that, she had rewritten herself.

And now?

Now it was time to return to the very scene that had once devoured her.

The boardroom. The Dragon's Den. Only this time, she wasn't walking in as prey.

By the time Maya pulled into the office parking lot, the chill of early spring still lingered in the air. The morning sun had started breaking through the clouds, casting long golden rays across the pavement, as if the world was gently waking up from its own winter. Her breath fogged briefly on the window, then faded.

Maya didn't grip the steering wheel like a lifeline. She just sat there for a moment, watching the sunlight stretch across the windshield. Her breath was slow, and her heart was steady.

This wasn't a battlefield anymore. This was just another beautiful day.

Her phone rang. It was Andrea. She picked it up.

"Morning, Andrea," she said warmly before her assistant could speak.

"Maya! You made it! The board meeting is today.

Are you ready?" she asked cautiously, with the memory of the last time still tucked in

the back of her mind.

"I am," Maya said calmly. "Let's make it a good day."

There was no panic or flinching in the air.

She saw the red bubbles on her phone.

Emails, messages, and alerts were all blinking for attention. She silenced them.

It is what it is. No need to panic. They could wait.

She stepped out of the car. The cold breeze nipped at her cheeks, crisp and clean, but the sunlight was soft against her skin. It kissed the edge of her collar and warmed her through her blazer. Her heels clicked across the pavement, but this time they didn't sound rushed. They sounded deliberate.

Inside, the office lobby was eerily quiet as always. The overhead lights cast a golden glow, mingling with the sunlight on the faces of the people arriving for work. Around her, coworkers shuffled in to start the day.

Maya smiled at the security guard. She stopped for a moment, read his name tag and said. "Good morning, Paul. How are you today?"

He blinked, surprised. "Uh, good. Thanks."

No wonder he was surprised. Maya had ignored him for years. It was a small gesture, but in a world of rush and anonymity, it might as well have been the first time Paul felt seen by someone in this building.

Maya's first stop, as always, was the coffee in the kitchen. She moved toward the machine and made herself a cup. The aroma swirled up, earthy and familiar. She didn't gulp it like a potion to survive the day, instead, she sipped it like a ritual, enjoying the taste and moment.

"Morning," said a voice beside her.

It was Adam, from finance. He was quiet but kind.

This time, Maya didn't brush past him.

"Morning, Adam. How was your weekend?" she said, and meant it.

His face lit up. "I spent it with my kids."

"Sounds magical," she smiled. And it did.

They exchanged a few more words about his kids and her vacation.

It was nothing profound, but it mattered for both of them.

She headed toward the boardroom.

Richard appeared right on cue.

"Morning, Maya," he said with his tone clipped. "You'd better bring your best today!"

She met his gaze cool, calm, and somehow untouchable.

"Good morning, Richard," she said, her voice even. "Let's do our best together!"

His eyebrows twitched. She was supposed to shrink, not shine. She smiled at him in confidence, walked past him, and entered the boardroom with grace.

The room was just as she remembered. Seven suits. Seven silences. Seven egos. Seven pairs of eyes are ready to judge.

But Maya didn't feel small. She felt ready.

She wore the same emerald-green blazer, but this time, it didn't feel like armor protecting her from complete exposure; it felt like a robe she chose, not to hide, but to honor herself.

Some noticed her and looked up. She didn't flinch. She went straight to the screen. Plugged in the laptop with no trembling fingers this time.

When Anita walked in and asked too loudly, "Trouble again, Maya?"

Maya smiled softly. "No, thank you, Anita. I got it under control."

And she did. The screen lit up. The men looked up. She stood firm.

"Good morning, everyone!" Her voice was calm.

"I won't waste your time," she began. "Here's what we need to see and why."

There were no cracks, no begging, and no tiptoeing.

As expected, the chairman was interrupting her.

"Can you explain it more in-depth, Maya?" She nodded once.

Not with fear, but with clarity. And she cut to the chase.

When the finance VP snapped, "The numbers seem incorrect!"

She met his challenge with grounded ease.

"I'd be happy to walk you through them in detail after the meeting.

But for now, let's stay focused on the bigger picture."

She set the pace.

She led the room.

And when the chairman said, "This feels safe," she didn't flinch. She smiled.

"Sometimes safe is smart. Especially when you're trying to turn a tanker, not a kayak."

A few faces twitched like they'd just swallowed their pride.

She didn't backtrack or apologize.

And when the final question came, sharp, skeptical, and dismissive, she didn't scramble.

She answered clearly, calmly, and convincingly. When she finished, there was silence.

"Thank you, Maya," said the chairman. She didn't feel the sensation of dismissiveness of the board. What she felt was acknowledgment for the first time.

Richard looked at her. His expression was unreadable.

But it didn't matter. Because she wasn't there for his approval.

She gathered her laptop without a rush and walked out with the same steps she entered with. She felt grounded, steady, and whole.

As she closed the heavy wooden door behind her, she didn't collapse. She exhaled.

Not because she had survived. But because she had owned it victoriously.

This time, she didn't crawl out of the dragon's den.

She walked with her head high like a woman with wings.

She didn't escape the dragons. She tamed them by showing

her worth.

33

MAYA WHO SAW

The hallway outside the boardroom was humming, same as always. Maya could hear the polished shoes clicking like metronomes of power and the faint hiss of the coffee machine with the constant undercurrent of performance.

She walked with calm steps. Her shoulders were back, her breath deep, and her heart steady. She was feeling on top of the world. Happy. Glorious. Like nothing could stop her now.

Just as she passed the glass-walled boardroom reception, she caught a flicker of something off. Anita sat behind the desk, usually perfect and polished, efficiently hammering away at her keyboard and a stare of 'I-am-the-boss here'. But now she was staring at the screen like she couldn't quite see it. Her fingers hovered above the keyboard, frozen. Her shoulders were hunched. The gloss had slipped. Her eyes were glassy. Her lips were pressed together in that dangerous way that holds back an avalanche.

Maya had almost passed her.

The old Maya would have gone by without noticing.

But now? She realized and turned back.

"Anita?" she said softly.

The woman startled slightly, blinking fast as if pulling herself together with sheer

force of will.

"Oh. Hi, Maya. Do you need something?"

Maya tilted her head. "No. Just … you look upset. Are you okay?"

Anita opened her mouth. Closed it. Tried to smile.

"I'm fine."

There was a pause.

Then she said it again. Quieter this time and less convincing.

"I'm fine."

Maya didn't buy it.

She slipped into a chair beside the desk, uninvited but entirely present.

"You don't look fine," she said.

Anita hesitated, blinked twice, and then, like a balloon finally giving out,

she deflated with a sigh. Her fingers dropped. Her voice came small.

"I'm just… having a rough day."

Maya leaned her hip gently against the counter. She didn't press. She waited. Anita looked at her, confused by the silence. The non-urgency. The presence. And suddenly, the words spilled out in a whisper.

"My mom is in the hospital. The doctors don't know if she will make it.

I barely slept. And Richard… well, Richard was being Richard this morning."

Maya nodded slowly. "I'm sorry."

Anita shook her head quickly, trying to pull herself back together.

"It's fine. I'm fine. Just ignore me."

But Maya didn't. She stayed right there. Because once, not that long ago, she had been Anita: tight-throated, over-functioning, running on fumes, holding back tears behind professionalism and polite smiles.

And someone had stopped for her. Maria. In a rain-soaked dining room. With breakfast. With a hug. With presence. Now it was her turn.

Anita continued with a voice like tissue paper. "It's just me. I'm the only child. My dad left years ago. I'm working here, trying to keep things together, and I don't even know how to ..."

Her voice broke. "I don't know how to do this alone."

Maya didn't think. She just moved. She stood, stepped around the desk, and wrapped Anita in a hug. Not the awkward kind. Not the polite-office kind. The real kind. The arms-around-someone's-soul kind. And as Anita shook in her arms, Maya closed her eyes and remembered when she was standing in Maria's kitchen and her overwhelming hug that made her crumble like a child as well and made her feel safe. It felt like being swallowed by a fire of kindness and understanding.

And now? She was that fire. That kindness. That understanding. Anita clung to her like a child to a ledge. Maya didn't say anything for a while. She just held her and let her cry. Let the tears fall without judgment. When Anita finally pulled back, her cheeks were blotchy, her eyes were red, and her usual strong voice had lost its strength.

"I'm sorry. I just ... I didn't mean to..."

Maya smiled, brushing a strand of hair from Anita's forehead.

"You don't have to apologize. We all fall apart sometimes."

Anita looked at her like she was seeing her for the first time.
"Why are you being so... nice?"

Maya smiled. "Because someone once was, when I didn't think I deserved it either."

There was a long pause. Then Maya did something she never would've imagined doing in her past life before coconuts, butterflies, and the island breeze.

She reached into her bag, pulled out a scrap of paper, the back of an old meeting note, and wrote down her address. She slid it across the desk.

"Here," she said. "I'm having a few people over in a couple of weeks.

Nothing fancy. Just some food, some laughter, and no suits allowed.

Come if you feel like it. I think it will do you good."

Anita stared at the note as if it had been written her address in a different language.

"You... want me to come to your house?"

Maya grinned. "Yes. Are you okay with that?"

Anita gave the smallest, most stunned nod Maya had ever seen.

"No one's ever invited me to something like that before here in the office."

Maya shrugged. "Well, maybe it's time someone did."

And for a moment, just a flicker, Maya saw the woman behind the professional mask. The tired heart. The scared daughter. The human being. The one who just needed to be seen. Like she once had.

Maya smiled. "See you next Friday, Anita."

34

THE TABLE SHE NEVER SET

Friday arrived. For the first time in years, Maya took the afternoon off. Not because she was sick. Not because she had crashed. Because she wanted to. A simple, radical act of claiming time and of choosing joy.

She kicked off her heels at the door and stepped barefoot into her apartment. Her space was still a bit chaotic, but it seemed cozier. Three weeks have already passed since she came back from the island. There were small reminders scattered throughout her apartment like the soap from the market she thought was a vegetable which was lying on the shelf in her bathroom like a sacrilege, the wooden blue butterfly from Maria in her bedroom which reminded her every single day of her strength, the necklace with the shell she has not been taken off since and a few spices in little jars in the kitchen that still carried the scent of the tropics. And today she was going to use them. She was going to cook. Once she was the guest at Maria's table, now she decided to be the host by herself. She laughed just thinking about it.

Me? Cooking! Voluntarily? I must be insane!

She went into the kitchen and started singing. With her rhythm came the dance. She slowly moved to the fridge to get out the food.

"Today I will cook for my friends," Maya said in silence, and remembered the night of the island bonfire. She remembered the mismatched chairs, the grilled plantains, the scent of spice and smoke in the air.

She remembered Maria's voice: "This is my joy. Let me feed you."

Now, it was Maya's turn. She rolled up her sleeves, tied her hair into a messy knot, and turned on a playlist with just enough salsa to make her hips sway. The kitchen came alive.

The chopping started awkwardly. The chili fought back. The coconut almost cost her a finger. But the mango slices looked right. The rice shimmered with saffron. She even remembered to stir the pot clockwise because Maria said it always infused the food with love.

"Maria, you'd be proud," Maya whispered aloud, her voice cracking with emotion.

"I'm feeding my friends tonight."

She paused and looked around. There was no one there, but she could feel her. Maria. It felt like she was sitting right next to her, watching over her. It seemed she shared with her the humming, the rhythm of chopping, the clatter of pots, the heat, the laughter, and the pure joy she experienced cooking for the first time.

The table she never used was dressed tonight in a patchwork tablecloth and mismatched plates. She put a row of candles in old jam jars. The scent of lime, coconut, and roasted sweet potato drifted through the apartment like a warm memory.

And then they arrived.

First, Gina, bursting in like sunshine with a bottle of wine and a squeal:

"You're really doing this?! Look at you, domestic goddess!"

Maya grinned and pulled her in. "Welcome to the new world order!"

Then came Emma, her sister, arms full of dessert and warnings about sugar.

Their mother followed stiffly and slightly confused by the setup, but holding a

small bouquet of flowers in her hand. "I didn't come for the food," she said.

"I came for you."

Andrea, her assistant, arrived next. She was more relaxed than Maya had ever seen her. "No agendas tonight!" she grinned.

And then Anita. The last person Maya ever imagined would cross her threshold. But here she was, holding a pie in a cracked plastic container and shifting from foot to foot like a child at her first sleepover.

"I didn't know if you meant it," Anita whispered.

"I did," Maya replied softly. And then, without thinking, she hugged her.

Anita stiffened and then melted.

"You're not alone anymore," Maya whispered.

The room was buzzing, a beautiful chaos of voices, scents, and music that wrapped around them like a warm embrace. The food was devoured. Laughter filled the corners. Emma and Gina started teasing each other like teenagers. Andrea was cracking open a second bottle of wine. Her mom was smiling.

And then there was a final knock at the door. Maya wondered

who was missing. But deep inside her, she knew the answer. Her heart jumped. She opened the door.

It was Ethan. Clean-shaven. No flowers. No bottle. Just him. It was strangely familiar. And that look he had. The one that says I'm not sure if I belong, but I hope I do.

"Hey," he said.

"Hey," she replied in a soft voice.

"I wasn't sure if you really wanted me here."

"I did," she said. "I really did."

She stepped aside to let him into the apartment. He entered.

The room quieted just enough for his presence to ripple. Gina gave Maya this secret look, saying: I know what is going on here. Ethan scanned the scene, the table, the food, the people, and then looked at her with a tenderness she hadn't seen in a long time.

"You did all this?"

She nodded, suddenly shy.

He smiled, stepping a little closer.

"You're glowing," he whispered.

And just like that, her whole body softened.

They didn't talk much that evening. But they didn't need to. He laughed at Gina's stories. Her mom rolled her eyes, listening to them. Emma offered parenting advice to Andrea. Just in case she needs it one day. Anita actually laughed, really laughed, at something Ethan said about the worst Zoom call of all time.

And Maya? She didn't hover. She didn't perform. She sat at the head of a table surrounded by people from different chapters of her life, work, family, and friendship. All of them are here. In one room. In one moment. And as candles flickered, forks clinked, and conversations bloomed, she felt something she hadn't felt in a long, long time.

Belonging. Not to a company. Not to a goal. Not to an image. But to herself. And to the wonderful mosaic of people who had seen her, helped her, challenged her, and stayed. She was surrounded by people she loved and who loved her, rooted in what truly matters.

She caught Ethan's eye from across the table. He raised his glass, just slightly. She smiled and raised hers in return.

And in that moment, under soft lights and surrounded by the people who had shown up, who cared for her, she wished Maria, Greg, Leo, and Gio would be here as well.

Maya felt something click into place.

She remembered the firelight from the island.

The taste of jackfruit.

The clink of bottles.

The stories shared.

The feeling of being seen.

That night, in her city apartment, far from the sea,

she recreated it without even realizing.

She had brought back a way of being.

Full of joy, rooted in who she was.

A type of presence that is with her even in difficult and painful moments.

She felt at peace.

Paradise, she now knows, is not a place to escape to.

It is the way you show up in the here and now.

She has discovered it far away on a remote island

and has uncovered that it has always been with her.

And now, she could hold that space for herself, and for others too.

The evening went by too fast. Everyone enjoyed it. Ethan as well.

He hugged her to say goodbye. Their hands found each other.
He looked her deeply in the eyes.
"It's different," he said. "You're different."
She looked at him. "Maybe I'm just more me."
He smiled again. "I like more you."
Her heart was full.
Maya stood in her doorway when he left.
She felt loved, at peace, and full of gratitude.
She felt riding the wave.
Maybe some stories aren't over yet.
Maybe some were just beginning.

IV

YOUR WHISPERING BUTTERFLY

"And you?
When will you begin
that long journey into yourself?"
Rumi

35

THE JOURNEY CONTINUES

Ready for more?

Visit www.whisperingbutterfly.com for exclusive behind-the-scenes content and updates on upcoming events. Feel free to share your story with the author and the community or sign up for the newsletter to hear insights that didn't make it into the book, and catch the next wave of inspiration.

Afterword

Sometimes, the life we build quietly becomes a cage, and we don't even notice until one day, we realize we don't know how to escape.

When I first started writing this book, I wasn't sure if I was building an escape hatch or a doorway. I only knew I needed to tell Maya's story because, in many ways, it was mine too. The constant rush, the quiet exhaustion, the gnawing question *"Is this all there is?"* had shaped Maya. And it has shaped me.

I wrote THE WHISPERING BUTTERFLY because I believe we all need a map back to ourselves. Not a map full of directions but full of invitations.

To get lost.

To listen.

To feel.

To remember.

This book didn't arrive fully formed. It unfolded the way we all do when we're learning a new way of being. The seed was planted 15 years ago, while I was living abroad completely out of my comfort zone, stumbling through a culture and language I barely understood. I was curious, listened, and learned. My personality was formed through many exotic experiences. Deep inside me, I knew: *One day, I'll tell this story.* Five years ago, the story truly began to take shape. On a trip to an island, we lived in a simple wooden lodge in the middle of the jungle, far from the tourist trails. Right next to us, by pure magic (or maybe destiny), a professional coach had rented the neighboring lodge. We spent hours talking about life, about meaning, about the things we forget in the rush of everyday living. Those conversations stayed with me. But life, full-time executive, full-time mom, swept me away again. Until now. Now, the time was right to bring Maya to life. Because finally, I had found myself. Untangled. In joy with who I was meant to be.

Although this story is fiction, every chapter, every encounter - the butterfly, the ants, the strangers, the ocean - mirrored real moments where I, too, began to see the world, and myself, differently.

Writing this story wasn't about perfect sentences or polished wisdom. It was about holding a mirror to the small moments, the ones that crack us open and quietly change something. I hope, somehow, it cracked something open in you, too.

If you find yourself standing at a crossroads, tired, restless, wondering, let me tell you: I see you. I've been you.

If you are asking yourself whether there's more to life than the next meeting, the next deadline, the next achievement...

There is. There always has been.

And now? It's your turn. Your time to pause. To question. To wander. (If you haven't already started.) To step off the beaten path and listen to the quieter voices inside you. The ones that have been waiting patiently, just beneath the noise, just beneath the expectations. You don't have to escape to a remote island to find your paradise.

Paradise isn't a place. It's a way of seeing. It's a way of choosing. It's already here, and you carry it within you.

Thank you for walking this journey with Maya.

Thank you for being brave enough to ask yourself, *"What if there's another way?"*

And if you hear a faint flutter, if something inside you stirs and dares to whisper, that's your butterfly, awakening too.

The story isn't over. It's just getting started.

You already know it. You're meant for more.

Hear the whisper and spread your wings,

Sabine MacDonald

About the Author

Sabine MacDonald was born in Germany, lives in Canada, and has always had a heart for the world. As an international executive, she led teams across Spain, Mexico, Brazil, Russia, the U.S., and beyond, living and working in seven countries, and traveling through more than 50. But her greatest journey wasn't a destination. It was rediscovering herself.

Today, she runs her own international consulting and coaching company, helping people transform across borders and reclaim their joy.

The Whispering Butterfly is her debut book: a soul-stirring story inspired by the real journeys that broke her open, brought her clarity, and reminded her of what truly matters.

You can connect with me on:
- https://www.whisperingbutterfly.com
- https://www.facebook.com/macdonald.sabine
- https://www.linkedin.com/in/sabine-macdonald
- https://www.instagram.com/macdonald_sabine

www.ingramcontent.com/pod-product-compliance
Lightning Source LLC
LaVergne TN
LVHW011326080426
835513LV00006B/212